AGAINST THE CARCERAL ARCHIVE

AGAINST THE CARCERAL ARCHIVE

THE ART OF BLACK LIBERATORY PRACTICE

Damien M. Sojoyner

FORDHAM UNIVERSITY PRESS   NEW YORK   2023

Fordham University Press has no responsibility for the persistence or accuracy of URLs for external or third-party Internet websites referred to in this publication and does not guarantee that any content on such websites is, or will remain, accurate or appropriate.

Fordham University Press also publishes its books in a variety of electronic formats. Some content that appears in print may not be available in electronic books.

Visit us online at www.fordhampress.com.

Library of Congress Cataloging-in-Publication Data available online at https://catalog.loc.gov.

Printed in the United States of America

25 24 23   5 4 3 2 1

First edition

To Elaine and Godfrey, whose love has always been unconditional.

To Shana, whose love has enabled me to reach levels I never thought possible.

To Naima and Nesanet, whose love gives my life true meaning.

Contents

Introduction   1

1   The Human and the Carceral Archival Project   17

2   Police and the Carceral Archival Project   32

3   Technology and the Social Sciences as Synergistic Violence   42

4   Environmental Instability   59

5   Policing Health and Safety   72

6   Liberation   81

Conclusion   93

Acknowledgments   103

References   107

AGAINST THE CARCERAL ARCHIVE

Introduction

During the summer of 2005, I had the good fortune to be able to work with and learn under the tutelage of Michael Zinzun. A former member of the Black Panther Party, Zinzun would be instrumental in the formation of the Coalition Against Police Abuse (CAPA) in Los Angeles, California. Applying the principles he learned while a member of the Panthers, Zinzun was adamant that study and planning were paramount to the strategic success of radical organizing. A reflection of such praxis, the CAPA headquarters were filled to the brim with a collection of magazines, books, academic journals, newspapers, VHS cassette tapes, flyers, and a wide array of audio, video, and written documentation. We spoke at length that summer, with me asking a bevy of questions, and with a laser focus, Zinzun maneuvered through the office space, able to pull the precise document or show me an old clip in support of his response.

Zinzun constantly stressed the importance of working in a collective fashion to develop plans that would account for the complexity of a multifaceted state apparatus. It was the planning, the study, the deep thinking that was of utmost importance to

Zinzun. While so much of organizing and activism had been reduced to marches and speeches, Zinzun stressed that various forms of active processes were needed in order to work against the carceral state and build anew. Although much of the emphasis within activism focused on the "doing," one of CAPA's main mandates was rigorous study. That was not an empty maxim. Since its inception, CAPA had been under constant state surveillance and had multiple forms of violence enacted upon it by state actors ranging from the Federal Bureau of Investigation (FBI) to the Los Angeles Police Department (LAPD). As a matter of strategy, study was emphasized as a means to both circumvent state action and actively work against the reproduction of violence that befell many people, organizations, and movements that were subsumed by or eliminated via the state during liberation struggles.

To this end, Zinzun placed great importance on theory as being a vital component of CAPA's core mission. This reference to theory was informed by his days in community and neighborhood reading groups where there was a meticulous engagement with a range of radical thinkers from around the world. Rather than promoting "theory for theory's sake," Zinzun pointed out that theory was key not only to digesting the varied possibilities of state reaction, but also to establishing a grounding for CAPA's work.

Thus, while CAPA as an organization was focused on the damage and violence caused by police to Black communities in Los Angeles, the analytic focus was not on the police as the prime directive. Rather, there was a multilayered analysis that explored the various points of inflection within the state apparatus, and as a result, such thinking situated the police as a formation of domestic warfare against Black people. Extending the analysis beyond Southern California, CAPA's aim was to expand beyond the limited scope of national imaginaries and understand the motivations and impulses of liberation efforts against carceral formations by Black communities throughout the African Diaspora. The major theorists of influence for Zinzun and many of his comrades were Black radical thinkers who positioned Blackness as the key interlocutor to understand matters of dispossession, violence, and enclosure as conducted under the auspices of state governance around the globe.

Building upon the core organizing principles of study and collectivity utilized by communal organizations such as CAPA, *Against the Carceral Archive* is a meditation on what I call the carceral archival project. The intellectual fodder for this meditative practice derives from five distinct collections housed at a critical node of liberation and communal praxis—the Southern California Library (SCL), located in Los Angeles. The framing of the text is situated within the reading group / collective / workshop format as described by Zinzun, which was foundational to the development of strategy, process, and action. Following the impulse of CAPA, the synthesis offered throughout the chapters is informed by provocations placed forth by Sylvia Wynter and Cedric Robinson. A primary aim is to distill the liberation efforts against the carceral state through a close reading of a set of archival collections as informed by Wynter and Robinson. Imagined as an open dialogue between the two master theoreticians, the arguments and ideas placed forth in the text are layered together to build a multifaceted rendering of the carceral archival project.

The Carceral Archival Project

The term *archive* is employed as both an analytic and a conduit to understand the material and ideological contestation between western epistemological traditions and Black communal knowledge production. The study of the archive as a source of power dynamics was most famously taken up by Michel-Rolph Trouillot, who wrote:

[T]he making of archives involves a number of selective operations: selection of producers, selection of evidence, selection of themes, selection of procedures—which means, at best the differential ranking and, at worst, the exclusion of some producers, some evidence, some themes, some procedures. Power enters here both obviously and surreptitiously. (Trouillot 2015, 53)

The matter of the archive as a study of colonial relationships, mythmaking, gendering processes, and site of imperial knowledge has been vital to understanding the multidimensionality of the archive beyond a site of objective knowledge formation (Spivak 1999; Chatterjee 2000). Importantly, recent scholarship on the shape and form of the archive as a mechanization that produces and arranges hierarchies and contains notable silences and omissions (both intentional and not) has been instructive in the reorientation and disruption of normative ontological imaginaries (Crawley 2017; Gordon 2017; Hartman 2007; Hicks 2010; Ferguson 2012; Fuentes 2010, 2016; Haley 2016; Sharpe 2016; Thomas 2019).

Building upon the range of theorizing upon the archive, the scope of the carceral archival project is informed by scholarship of critical geographers who have worked to situate the dynamics between and among formations of material and ideological exploitation and Black people within the context of epochs that are defined by a set of specific political, social, and economic contexts (Gilmore 2007; McKittrick and Woods 2007; Woods 2017; Wilson 2019). Read from such a vantage point, carcerality as the dominant modality of state governance in the United States developed during the 1960s in direct parallel with the ascension of militarism as the primary expression of statecraft as a means to buttress the massive fissures gaping throughout an inept capitalist infrastructure. Ruth Wilson Gilmore explains the significance of this moment in the following terms:

The years 1967–68 also marked the end of a long run-up in annual increases in profit, signaling the close of the golden age of U.S. capitalism. The golden age had started thirty years earlier, when Washington began the massive buildup for World War II. The organizational structures and fiscal authority that had been designed for New Deal social welfare agencies provided the template for the Pentagon's painstaking transformation.... It changed from a periodically expanded and contracted Department of War to the largest and most costly bureaucracy of the federal government. The United States has since committed enormous resources to the first permanent warfare apparatus in the country's pugnacious history.

... Indeed, the U.S. welfare state has been dubbed "military Keynesianism" ... to denote the centrality of war-making to socioeconomic security. On the domestic front, while labor achieved moderate protections against calamity and opportunities for advancement, worker militancy was crushed and U.S. hierarchies achieved renewed structural salience. (Gilmore 2007, 25–26)

Bleeding through all aspects of state governance, militarism—most readily identifiable at the point of conflict outside the borders of the nation-state—was further intensified and unleashed within the borders of the United States and took the shape of carcerality. Given its immediate proximity to militarism, carcerality is defined as an epoch of domestic warfare that informs the logics of state structures and sociality within the United States (Rodríguez 2021). Impressive in scope, carcerality as an ideological endeavor became the dominant expression of state life and informed the development of virtually all state structures such as education, health, law, housing, and employment. The carceral archival project as an analytic framework seeks to cull through the various terrains of ideological and material manipulation via (the often violent) expressions of statecraft. Given the inherent disposition of the state to violently impose hierarchal structures via its archival capacity, a rendering of carcerality as an archival modality provides a framework to study the breadth of the carceral state.

Thus the carceral archival project functions as a constitutive difference-making generator that bifurcates between life and non-life or, as will be taken up later, between human and nonhuman. Advancing Trouillot's argument, the exclusionary capacity of the carceral archival project is in the ability to create particular types of civil subjects and the destruction/eradication/erasure of other subjects. Immersed within the logics of racial capitalism, the carceral archival project is guided by ideological and material mechanizations that are fueled by and demand allegiance to pejorative blackness—the making and reproduction of philosophical, moral, ethical, and ontological processes that denigrate, suppress, and attempt to create Blackness within a narrow framework that in turn provides the legitimization and facilitation of vile processes of gross exploitation and violence.

Most commonly expressed through ascriptions of individual subjects (which are connected to manufactured notions of freedom), the actual administration of the carceral archival process is facilitated through the ideological conscription to pejorative blackness via state structures. Taking on a variety of titles and names depending on the prescribed national and/or regional designation (such as justice, housing, health, education), the archival capacity is revealed in the making of the ontological practices that erase the hand of the state in the facilitation of racialized violence. Thus, the meting out of rewards and suppression takes on the logic of individualized choices and moral actions that are in congruence with a set of civil principles. Pulling back the veil ever so slightly from such a charade reveals that said principles are a crude form of alchemy intended to fortify the legitimacy of the carceral state while also masking the vile processes of violence that are inherent within the very state structures upholding the carceral state's legitimacy.

The violence imbricated within the carceral archive process is a reflection of the Sisyphean task of maintaining legitimacy/normality in the face of non-life-sustaining ontological practices. Specifically, the carceral state must make illogical the life-affirming social visions emanating from Black communal epistemes. An arduous task, the archival process is in a consistently reactionary posture with respect to Black manifestations of life and possibility. State structures, the civic articulation of ideological and material violence, are the primary vehicle through which the reaction against Black social visions manifests. Within the context of the modern carceral era, state structures perform a critical archival role in attempting to legitimize violence. The vast array of data, knowledge production, and resources housed within and utilized by state structures provide the war chest that enables the state to violently respond to formations of Black liberation and life.

Constructed as a benefit for the linear advancement of civilization, the archival management by state structures provides a means to refine technologies of violence and suppression that manifest through the logics of a militaristic carceral synergistic practice. Indebted to a genealogical practice that is predicated upon difference-making as the driver of civic belonging, the philosophical underpinnings of state structures within the carceral epoch work to make Black social visions a threat to the civic project and thus necessary of erasure/eradication. As such, the carceral archive scheme operates not merely within the purview of the physical warehousing of people behind bars and in cages, but via the articulation through a vast structural network. Thus, as the dominant model of state governance, carcerality is the connective logic that bleeds through structures that in turn are foundational to the civic project (such as housing, education, health care, science, and the law).

Southern California Library

The Southern California Library (SCL) is many things to many people. For some it is a respite from the trials of traversing the labyrinth of the carceral state. A momentary breather, a place to sit and be, a sanctuary of bodily and spiritual nourishment. For others, it is an intellectual haven that is on par with some of the greatest repositories in the world. While the collections are disparate in their content—ranging from the International Union of Oil Workers to audio recordings of 1950s and '60s rhythm and blues singers—it is the energy of labor and love that resonates throughout the collections. Such liberatory possibilities can be found in the origins of the library. Founded by Emil Freed in the wake of the Red Scare that disrupted the lives of so many, the SCL provided a safe space to house the work of those whose lives were being uprooted out of fear of state retaliation.

It was during this time that SCL became much more than an archival depot; it soon became a critical site of meeting, organizing, and planning against the targeted militaristic aims of western state governance. It is this complex overlay of the past and the present that the current stewards of SCL, Yusef Omowale and Michele Welsing, have inherited and built upon. SCL is located in the heart of South Central Los Angeles, and over the course of the past roughly twenty years, Yusef and Michele have expanded the library beyond the physical walls, crafting the physical and metaphorical space to become an extension of the neighborhood and an intellectual and political hub of organizing and thinking. Through efforts ranging from tenants' rights and reproductive justice organizing to political education of young people and schoolteachers, SCL has been central in crafting the communal imaginary of liberation.

A key part of the fabric of the surrounding community and the larger Black community of Los Angeles, SCL has been keen on the development of innovative methodological approaches to the documentation, preservation, and strategic utilization of the lived Black Angelino experience. Given the extreme pressures of the carceral state that have forced many Black people out of the city and county limits, such work is of the utmost importance. In tandem with vast collections such as that of the Los Angeles chapter of the Black Panther Party, the Charlotta Bass collection, the Coalition Against Police Abuse Collection, and several other radical Black organizing collectives, SCL is home to a dynamic repository of knowledge formation and production that is critical to the study and planning needed to understand both the inner workings of the carceral state and nuanced strategies toward liberation.

A primary aim of this book is to sit with the radical genealogical ontological praxis that flows through the collections of the Southern California Library. One of the key facets of such praxis is the great importance placed on studying. Such studying reveals the incongruence among thoughts and plans. Rather than shying away from such tensions, my inclination is to lean into the source of the tension as a way to understand the multiplicity of possibilities that in turn crafted organizing strategy. Such a philosophical orientation reveals a complex and dynamic rendering of the carceral state. There are no simple fixes and there is always an eye toward identifying modes of cooption and neutralization. What emerges from the archive is a multifaceted rendering of the carceral state that extends beyond the walls of the prison and manifests within key forms of governmentality in regimes throughout the world. As an intervention within the study against the carceral state, my aim is to center the work of the Southern California Library and key collections housed at the library to better understand and plan against carcerality as a modality of governance, ideology, and material reality.

Perhaps the best way to center SCL is through the manner in which it locates itself as a site of study, community, and building. Informed by a broad genealogical cadre of Black Studies scholars, the library has claimed the name "fugitive archive" to situate itself alongside the archival collections. Speaking to fugitivity, there is a request by SCL for patrons to sign a use agreement in the spirit of collectivity and struggle that is central to the building of the collections within SCL. The use agreement is focused on a framework that centers the collections as a site of fugitive Black study. To that end, SCL does not look to claim ownership over the collections.

Statement of Fugitive Archive, Southern California Library

Fugitive Archives

We are a fugitive archive—an acknowledgement that we are unprofessional, lack capacity, illegitimate, with no histories worth preserving. Almost criminal. We have already been forgotten. Our invisibility is threatening. There is strength in this position of dismissal.

Fugitivity is not an act of escape or strategy of resistance. It is defined first and foremost as a practice of refusing the terms of negation and dispossession that are offered as our only inheritance.

It is a grappling with precarity, while refusing these terms of impossibility with an active commitment to creating alternative futures.

Fugitivity is a refusal to be refused. An unwillingness to know our place, and instead engaging possibilities to live unbounded lives. Mobilizing the everyday as sites of refusal.

Fugitivity as a practice emphasizes mobility, resistance, and expressiveness. We work to exploit the limits of the permissible, to inhabit transient spaces of freedom.

Fugitive archives are not just a people's history of the same country, but a movement against the possibility of a country.

Located in everyday imaginings and becoming, fugitive archives deal with the troubled, disaffected, unruly, and unwilling. Those who cannot be forgiven because they do not seek redemption.

We are a refuge for those who are denied spaces to exist; for those who do not have answers, but are working on questions.

Ultimately, the fugitive archives are willing to burn. The ashes will still provide a way.

The fugitive archives engage:

Quiet

Not a passive act, but a way of being. A practice of refusal. A means to care for our interiorities, to connect with the power of the erotic. Creating the preconditions for deep listening and reflection.

Vulnerablity

Intimacies on display—always at risk of being interrupted, overheard, seen, captured.

Improvisation

Not invested in what is, we are better able to repurpose what we have to invent what we need. And what we can find, we will claim and use. Because there is nothing that has not been made from our limbs and histories. And because what has been taken has been forgotten, some will call it stealing, but we don't care. Survival has its costs.

Forgetting, misremembering

We forget our proper names and positions. We salvage safety from not remembering where we were, what we did, or what happened.

We engage the fissures and gaps that emerge when we refuse the truth of the official version. We do not recall our contributions or heroic deeds, allowing us to reclaim our complex selves; a place where homemaking is possible.

In the end, we are more faithful to the possibility of freedom than the facts.

Southern California Library Use Agreement

The archives are dangerous. We cannot save you from this past that is not past. We cannot protect you from the pain of remembering what is meant to be forgotten. Entering here requires an engagement with landscapes of suffering. It is a journey towards death. This history is killing you too. You are implicated in this story.

This content is authorized for creating new possibilities of living. Any other use is a violation of our collective labor for freedom. Reproduction alone will not end the violence. Using what is found here to exhibit criminalized bodies without humanity, and heroes pursuing matters of inclusion, can result in severe logics of punishment and social death for those unjustly marked by difference.

You may not find what you are looking for. But you will be responsible for what you make, share, and leave behind. Access to intimate details of what it is to resist brutality requires a practice of mindfulness, careful listening, and creativity.

By joining these memories, you are committing to a shared responsibility of:

Learning from, rather than just about these histories.
Seeing beyond what is, to what can be.
Only disrupting the dead for the sake of the living.
Taking care of yourself, and others, along the way.

You cannot steal this. It has already been stolen and returned. This archive was abandoned and found long ago. You cannot steal this, it is already yours.

It is not our desire to track and account for how this archive is used and shared. We seek no credit. But there is a cost to caring for what was to be destroyed. We have long borne the costs of making this available, and we hope that you will share in that debt with us.

There is not time to tell you everything. We trust that you will remember.

The Archive and the Collections

The framing of the carceral archival project is informed by five collections housed at the Southern California Library. A hub of communal organizing and intellectual development, SCL houses a vast range of collections and is home / workspace / creative inspiration for community members, organizers, and teachers. Four of the collections—Los Angeles Chapter of the Black Panther Party, Coalition Against Police Abuse, Urban Policy Research Institute, and Mothers Reclaiming Our Children—are the holdings of communal organizing that simultaneously pushed back against the violent encroachment of the state into the lives of Black people and offered pathways to the creation of sociality based upon tropes of common humanity. The fifth collection is that of geographer and Black Studies scholar Clyde Adrian Woods, whose work positions Black ontologies as the rational modality of life in the face of decadent western epistemological traditions that demanded ruthless adherence.

This meditation upon the carceral archival project is based upon the wide range of textual documentation housed within

the aforementioned collections. The records of the five collections indicate that the struggle against state repression identified the vast arrangement of surveillance mechanisms, prisons,
police, criminal courts, probation and parole officers, general
enclosure, and the material and ideological itinerants that bled
through all state structures as the dominant form of governance.
As a result, significant energy was devoted to understanding the
many facets of state manipulation and terror. A serious amount of
time—study—was allocated to thinking, reading, and engaging
collectively in a concerted effort to bring in textual material from
a variety of sources to process the intent and scope of new developments within state governance. What I refer to as the carceral
archival project was representative of an epistemological tradition
dedicated to the reinforcement of hierarchies as the modality of
social arrangements. While it was a new formation with respect
to its scope, it was read by the creators of these collections as a
part of a broader set of political contestations that attempted to
stymie Black liberation. Perhaps most important, the study was
rigorous—organizing collectives participated in reading groups
and conducted workshops and symposiums that engaged with
complex planning documents; dense political, economic, and
social theory; and rich historical material.

The carceral archival project as an analytic framework is situated within an understanding of the state as derived from the
depths of a western intellectual tradition that is indebted to the
logics of a permanent bifurcation (such as good/bad, heaven/
hell, black/white). Rather than being an exception to western
knowledge production, the carceral archival project fits squarely
into a reactionary genealogy that has employed a wide array of
perverse mythical tropes to rationalize violent difference-making hierarchies as normative expressions of sociality and state
governance.

Against the Carceral Archive is structured as an engagement
with the collections as a method to understand the many facets

of the carceral archive project. The first chapter is a theoretical orientation that locates the major tenets of dominant western epistemological traditions and situates the carceral archival project as the logical conclusion of such production. The subsequent chapters (2–6) are brief treatises upon the major themes that develop out of the collections in relationship to the carceral archive project: policing, technology, environment, health, and liberation. Each of the chapters introduces a brief archival moment taken from the collections to provide entrée into the social and political milieus that inform the precarious dynamics between state governance and Black life. The conclusion includes a small representation of documents housed within the collection at SCL. In the spirit of Black collective traditions, my hope is that this book can be utilized as a reference and intellectual tool to assist in the contestation of carcerality and to contribute, even in the most modest fashion, toward the liberation of Black communities.

1

The Human and the Carceral Archival Project

The state demands its pound of flesh, but first, the state needs adherence. Adherence is a colonial enterprise that makes large fissures seemingly disappear. This is a forced contrivance that has both ideological and material consequences. One of the first tasks of a colonial enterprise was (and continues to be) to form structures that provided the bureaucratic means to establish state authority. These structures came in various amalgamations and schemes but were created as a conduit to facilitate the extraction of capital from a "found land" to the host of hyperexploitation: racial capitalist nation formations. Virtually all colonial enterprises, including the British, Dutch, Spanish, Portuguese, and French, were indebted to such models as a means to justify brutal exploitation.

The names of these structures varied across colonial regimes, but in general they targeted similar categories of capital-based extraction: land, people, material goods, and the meting out of discipline. One of the central tasks of these state-based structures was to reorganize the governing logic of knowledge production that informed ways of being. A totalizing ontological endeavor, the scope of these structures sought to erase established episte-mologies and subsequently legitimate western racial capitalist modalities that were governed by strict hierarchical sensibilities predicated upon violent notions of difference.

As constituted, state structures have been central to the man-ufacturing and maintenance of myths to maintain brutal regimes of exploitation and terror. The myth becomes vital to the promul-gation of nation-building as it forms an ideological buffer against knowledge formations that expose its origins as vile fantasy. La-beled as heresy or conspiracy, these knowledge traditions trouble the taken-for-granted philosophical tenets of western intellectual traditions. A brief excavation of western ontological genealogies reveals the totality of myths that western knowledge constructs and how the very formation of western thought is based upon patterns of erasure. The construction of history as a social fact is imbricated within a western tradition that is based upon fabri-cation. As articulated by Cedric Robinson,

> Throughout much of the human past, what we now take as the natural linear construction of history would have been taken as an aberration. Among some people, for in-stance, we are told that until recently there were not even words in their languages for the past, the present, and the future, the critical integuments of our linear conception of history. Instead, time was measured by phases of the moon (among the Babylonians), the appearances of stars (Egyptians), climatic seasons, the reigns of monarchs and emperors (in Europe through the High Middle Ages), and other recurrent spectacles which confirmed the cyclical structure of life. And history, most frequently discontin-uous fragments from the past, adhered to these diverse chronological parameters. . . .
>
> This peculiarity is barely disguised in the Western escha-tological ordering of history. Modern Western civilization

> derives from its cultural predecessor, Judeo-Christianity, a notion of secular history which is not merely linear but encompasses moral drama as well. (Robinson 2019, 6)

Robinson argues that at the heart of dominant western epistemological projects, the constructed narrative of history as a matter of reason and fact was informed by very particular western Christian imbrications of space and time as a means to assert authority over competing traditions that were much more egalitarian in their formation and implementation. Placing Robinson in conversation with Sylvia Wynter, we can understand that the construction of history along these linear tropes was crucial to the development of a human project that was predicated upon the building of specific western knowledge traditions that were invested within modalities of gross exploitation. The human project as described by Wynter was part of a philosophical reckoning that enabled the binary positionality of western Christian dogma to be continued into western epistemological processes that undergird modern rational thought or what Robinson refers to as the structure of the mind. Wynter states,

> This "enormous act of expression/narration" was paradoxical. It was to be implemented by the West and by its intellectuals as indeed a "Big Bang" process by which it/they were to initiate the first gradual de-supernaturalizing of our modes of being human, by means of its/their re-invention of the theocentric "descriptive statement" Christian as that of Man in two forms. The first was from the Renaissance to the eighteenth century; the second from then on until today, thereby making possible both the conceptualizability of natural causality, and of nature as an autonomously functioning force in its own right governed by its own laws (i.e., *cursus solitus naturae*) (Hubner 1983; Blumenberg 1983; Hallyn 1990), with this, in turn, making possible the cognitively emancipatory rise and gradual development

of the physical sciences (in the wake of the invention of Man1), and then of the biological sciences (in the wake of the nineteenth century invention of Man2). These were to be processes made possible only on the basis of the dynamics of a colonizer/colonized relation that the West was to discursively constitute and empirically institutionalize on the islands of the Caribbean and, later, on the mainlands of the Americas. (Wynter 2003, 263–64)

Situated as a conversation, Wynter and Robinson's dialogue pushes for an understanding of the construction of modern western epistemology as effaceable in its formation. The processes of vast erasure that have been at the heart of western knowledge traditions have been necessary to maintain the normative, violent logics of exploitation that have been the generative underbelly of western thought. Given the expansion of western epistemological traditions into the modern turn, Wynter and Robinson provide insight into two critical aspects of western ontological development: (1) The inherent bourgeois sensibility that was a marked characteristic of dominant western thought which functioned to minimize/contain/erase ontologies that condemned the normalization of exploitation; and (2) The permanent situating of Blackness into the realm of the nonhuman as a key component of philosophical traditions that serve as the intellectual underbelly of western imperialism.

Robinson notes that the formation of western thought is riddled with bourgeois conceits that reveal the lengths to which central western theorists went to erase radical formations:

Similarly, the elevation of natural law philosophy by renegade medieval scholars into a formidable opposition to private property, racism, and imperialist excess was neglected. The alternative discourses, both of the ancient world and of the seventeenth and eighteenth centuries, were directly implicated in the legitimation of slave economies, slave labor, and racism. Democracy, too, fueled by centuries of popular resistances, had acquired its better champions among medieval socialists. Notwithstanding their keen appetites for history, Marx and Engels had chosen to obliterate the most fertile discursive domain for their political ambitions and historical imaginations. (Robinson 2019, 115–16)

Robinson's argument of the knowing erasure of knowledge traditions that emanated from within Europe itself is critical to understanding the motivations and instincts of an intellectual system that went to (and continues to go to) great lengths to mask ontological practices that counter the normalization of violent difference-making hierarchies.

Firmly established within exploitative hierarchies, western intellectual thought positioned Blackness outside the realm of human. As posited by Wynter,

In the wake of the West's second wave of imperial expansion, pari passu with its reinvention of in Man now purely biologized terms, it was to be the peoples of Black African descent who would be constructed as the ultimate referent of the "racially inferior" Human Other, with the range of other colonized dark-skinned peoples, all classified as "natives," now being assimilated to its category—all of these as the ostensible embodiment of the non-evolved backward Others—if to varying degrees and, as such, the negation of the generic "normal humanness," ostensibly expressed by and embodied in the peoples of the West. (Wynter 2003, 266)

As articulated by Wynter and Robinson, the development of western intellectual traditions was based upon a set of philosophical conditions that condemned radical ontological practices. Given the expansion of western thought through violent imperialistic endeavors, the imperative of western thought was to situate Black ontological practices as nonhuman and thus remove such traditions from the realm of rational thought.

On Ideology

A key feature of the interplay between Wynter and Robinson is the manner in which they expose the creation of linear times-capes. Through painstaking detail, Wynter and Robinson demonstrate that the creation and invocation of western ontological derived notions of theory were central to the demarcation of one given period from another. Formulated in a linear fashion, the intended reading of western theoretical traditions is to substantiate the advancement of "human" thought. The result of such a framing provides the basis for the conceptualization of history—a fabrication of western thought that separates time, people, and space based upon racialized markers of distinction. As noted by Robinson on history as an ontological anomaly, "The linear notion of history is consequently rather unique in human consciousness." (Robinson 2019, 6) Thus, Wynter and Robinson's conversation underlay the significance of theory as the mortar that binds linear thinking to western timescapes.

While theory as a tool of ontological manipulation is vital to western intellectual traditions, ideology animates theory as a governing logic of sociality. Although the modern inflection of theory has been credited with the move toward the material (via the human) and away from the metaphysical (thus the ideological), the difference-making projects that were central to western ideological mythmaking strategies are the same philosophical precepts that informed the modern turn. Specifically, the ontological chisel that was vital to the violent cutting of rigid binary religious modalities into large swaths of premodern "European" subjects was employed to create a particular type of modern racialized, gendered, and sexed European consciousness.

Just as vital as the imposition of violent hierarchical religious dogma was the attempted erasure of ideological manifestations (such as metaphysical practices) that did not align with binary sensibilities. In this manner, ideology proved to be a consistent thorn in the side of a burgeoning western ontological practice. Such a practice was immersed in the construction of mythical tropes that reified power within the hands a few rather than well-practiced ideological models that distributed cultural, material, and intellectual resources among the masses. In this regard, ideology is important.

While developed on the soil of the European hinterland, the inclination for erasure was central to the western epistemological reaction to Black ontological traditions. One of the central aspects of modernity and the direct by-product of theory was to erase Black ideological practices. Either configured into a barely recognizable form that removed radical sensibilities or vanquished as outlier / illegible / unintelligible / lesser form / nonexistent, the effect was to mute the collective ethos that was at the heart of said ontological engagements. Yet, while the effort sought to diminish Blackness, a central task for theory was to make the matter a *fait accompli*. Through grand pronouncements about human sociality and the nature of the world and life in general, the erasure of Black ontological practices from these exaggerated, bloated statements of racialized propaganda under the guise of theory sought to make western modalities appear omniscient. Yet, as many a plantation owner and prison warden learned at the hands of unrelenting revolt, Black ontological practices did not disappear, and thus Black ontological practices continue to be a foil to western epistemological directives that seek to suppress life.

It is from this purview that the ideology as a basis of consciousness was central to the modern turn and thus was deeply embedded within the formulation of theory (as derived from the human) as the driver of European ontological traditions. Thus, the supposed rationality of theory is merely a cover for western ideological presuppositions that attempt to enforce adherence to violent-making binary logics that work to suppress specific groupings of people and ontological practices. The importance of theory within this equation is the establishment of governance strategies that have facilitated the imposition of state structures as markers of human achievement/existence. As a result, western-informed ideology has become the invisible undercurrent through which state structures manifest.

State Structures and Ideology

With respect to Blackness, the material and ideological subjection of Black ontological practices as nonhuman was facilitated via state structures. Specifically, state structures attempted to make the state legible as a legitimate formation of adherence while simultaneously making illegible formations whose core tenets opposed and/or followed different routes than the exploitative contours of western epistemological traditions. Absent state structures, demands of adherence to the state are absurd. There is no logical coherence to its provincial authority, and moreover, the multiple borders the state attempts to patrol are illogical to epistemological traditions that offer vastly differing understandings of life, land, and social relationships.

Within the contemporary state apparatus, carcerality is the dominant mode of governance, and a main imperative of the carceral state is to make life legible through an archival process. State structures such as the Department of Justice, Department of Corrections, and Division of Juvenile Affairs work as a dual processor with respect to the mechanism of state power—governing the logics of belonging and the human. These structures provide the material, moral, and scientific justification of state claims to govern the social, cultural, and political function of the citizenry. Importantly, it is through this function that these structures make legible the terms of the citizen within the confines of the state.

It is thus here at the key juncture of forming the contours of the citizen that legibility is understood as one of the central aspects of the carceral archival project: the ability to make legible notions of belonging and the human upon the structuring guidelines of these voracious state structures.

State structures animate the limited confines of the western imperial project as the sole arbitrator for which claims to land, culture, and social engagement are articulated. Resting within the very rigid lines of western civic epistemological traditions, any expression of belonging to the nation is predetermined by historical processes that are governed according to ideological precepts that demand the attenuation to hierarchies and difference. Not stable in its formation, such a process is reactionary in its development schema in such a way that very little is stable other than the need to constantly make hierarchies real. State structures are constructed in a limited fashion in an effort to prevent the possibility of dissent. Any and every potential epistemological tradition that goes in a different direction than the precepts of the governing edict of the state structure is made illegible the very moment it appears within the social arrangement established by the archive-making capacity of state governing structures. It is within this milieu that claims of belonging are predetermined by a structural arrangement that has been designed to mute the irrationality of hierarchies.

The limited scope of the carceral archival project reveals the secondary power-making aspect of state structures. Given that the structures operate both to make legible, but importantly, to render that which is illegible, the very function of these structures is to govern the logics of the human. Reinforcing difference as the conduit of sociality and governance, the ethos of these state structures is to make very particular claims about the human. In accordance with the mythical precepts of racial capitalism, the human process rests within the supposed rupture of the rational from the divine. It is on the basis of this rupture that state structures are then able to generate the authority to proclaim legibility. The rupture, or the *myth* of rupture, is the key ontological device that allows modernity to sweep away the vile and violent reality of western imperialism.

Yet while encumbered by the focus on rational thought and scientific development, a cursory dive into the logistics of the rupture reveals a preoccupation with the archiving of the human that reified the logics of difference. The pillars of western intellectual governance, from lineages of monarchs throughout Europe to enlightened thinkers, were fixated upon making the human the linchpin of difference-making processes. The extent to which philosophical treatises and state edicts alike went to justify the ordering of human life would be laughable if not for the animation of such a historical past which is readily apparent in similar proclamations of contemporary state governance.

The ideological trick that state structures employ is the continual making and remaking of their existence as vital to the function of a healthy democratic polity. There is a demand to believe that without the existence of Departments of Justice or Corrections, social, political, and economic relationships would degenerate into a permanent state of chaos. In a vicious feedback loop, laws and policy that embolden state structures are passed in the name of protecting a social arrangement that is predicated upon the violent buttressing of hierarchies. Consequently, the passage of these laws affirms the sanctity of an Aristotelian democratic tradition that informs the hierarchical difference-making techniques critical to western imperialism.

The circuits of such a loop are continually powered by a reaffirmation of the human as the critical component that must be enhanced and refined. The historical record of western civilization is littered with boundless case studies of bizarre and absurd attempts to perfect the human. Understanding the human as an ongoing project is to read the human as entity/formation/experiment that was designed to be constantly improved. The ideological underpinning of such a belief is guided by a set of models upon which the ideal human is based. These models are not static, yet while their dynamisms are attributed to technological development or intellectual enhancement, they emanate from the instability of an ideological arrangement that demands adherence to hierarchies. Clinging to the fragility of their existence (that is, belief within), the very existence of the human is in constant flux. Teetering on the edge of legitimacy, state structures are critical cogs either to reify old modalities (usually through means of violent repression) or to promote the palatable discourse of extremely distorted traditions (via gross cooptation) that excise the human as the central aspect of social relationships.

Returning to the great rupture, the transition has been marked by the advent of rational thought that led to a more precise manner of understanding the world and thus science. Yet, omitted from such a mythical narrative are the countless knowledge formations from within the borders of what is now considered Europe that contested the basis of hierarchies central to the imperialist goals of monarchs and burgeoning capitalists alike. Such traditions had to be excised from the linear retelling of history or else they would threaten the very conceptualization of the human. Rather than reckon with the multiple possibilities of life outside of a limited binary formation, the divine was mocked, yet not removed. The violent hierarchies that facilitated the difference-making projects of western Christendom were central to the binary code found throughout the great scientific paradigm shift. The material realities that undergirded imperial religious practices did not diminish; rather, they slowly became hidden underneath the façade provided by state structures. Operating within the proverbial shadows and outside of the governance model of scientific rationality, the moral impetus key to hierarchical formations of Western Christendom became central to the political, economic, and social edicts by which state structures adjudicated the terrain of modern humanity.

Similarly, the basic tenets of western imperialism during the nadir of the modern turn were indebted to a fixation of the human as the ideological project upon which difference would always be made real. It was at this moment that state structures became the logical purveyors of difference and thus virtually all processes of the civic project writ large became tainted by the stench of western epistemological infatuation with mapping difference upon every facet of social relationships. Such a dynamic is perhaps most clearly understood within the logics of an ideological precept responsible for upholding the moral and intellectual contours of difference-making projects—the law. A loosely based concept with a singular focus on the making and remaking of the human as an entity worthy of ascription, the law was and continues to be a set of mythical standards that are reactionary in nature and fleeting in terms of value (outside of very particular material rendering of value) or regard for the sanctity of life.

The Law and State Structures

While the common reference to law invokes processes of the formal juridical realm of the state, it is important to note the significance of the modern scientific utilization of law as a marker of material fact. Ranging from the laws of nature to laws of social arrangements, the totalizing effect of the law is not only to be descriptive (as in what is possible), but also to serve as a tool of erasure (to remove all that is not possible). The law, as an ideological device, was and continues to be critical in the configuration of the human as a centerpiece of state governance. State structures, as the articulator of the law, make legible the boundaries of the human and tirelessly work to prevent the exposure of the mythical nature of law as a matter of ideology and thus tear asunder the human project as a model of lived human existence.

The genealogical framework of the law as a precondition of the human reveals that rather than a gift of modernity, it is indebted to western Christendom as a technique of governance. Yet, it was modernity that allowed law to transition from the mouth of the western church to the faceless realm of amorphous state structures. This shift reflected the scientific rationality of the limited democratic project that emboldened the state to become the arbiter of that which was legible—human. Within this framework, the state now possessed the authority to govern both the sacred and the scientific. Informed by ideological precepts of the western church, the sacred provided authority over matters of moral and ethical dominion. The scope of the law thus provides the state with the scientific and moral standing to effectively map out the contours of the human. State structures are thus the dominion by which the law becomes provincial rule and establishes authority to codify the realm of human.

State structures within this arrangement are critical to the reification of difference as the barometer by which social arrangements exist. During the modern turn the ensconcement of difference within the logics of the human became attuned to Blackness as the terrain of demarcation. State structures became charged with providing the ideological, and by extension theoretical, proof to enshrine blackness as a pejorative object for which the continuation of the human project would expand. While such structures have a bureaucratic component and function, it is indeed the bureaucratic nature of these structures that renders them indispensable to the maintenance of the human. These structures have become the basis upon which grand principles of western existence rest: liberty, justice, freedom. The parsing of these bureaucratic functions from their ideological roots is an impossible task and as a result, these state structures have become central to the state. As an anecdote, the Department of Justice does not simply represent the administrative capacity of the state; it has become interwoven into a mythical narrative that demonstrates the supposed democratic nature of western traditions. In this manner, it embodies both the material/scientific and the sacred.

The logic of policies, rulings, and structuring of the dissemination of the rule of law is protected by the incorruptibility of scientific methodologies. The tenor of those same policies, rulings, and structuring is emboldened by a moral standard on par with the incorruptibility of the divine. Thus, any call to dismantle or abolish the Department of Justice is not merely trimming the fat of a bureaucratic structuring mechanism. It is calling for a reckoning of western epistemological traditions. In a clever sleight of hand, the positioning of the ideological work of the human project within the realm of state structures makes the call for undoing the violence appear irrational. The normalization of modernity's greatest gifts—scientific reasoning and democratic-based ethical tenets—has made the violent structuring of difference upon Blackness as natural as the sun rising or the breathing of air.

It is in the framing of the intimate relationship among state structures and the human project that we come to understand that one of the central functions of state structures is the reproduction of the ontological conditions that normalize violence upon Black subject making. These structures are the shiny façade of the human project that simultaneously provide shelter for the archiving of human difference that is crucial to the maintenance of violence upon Black subject making.

Data and the Human

Within the confines of the sheltered space, science becomes critical. Specifically, the shift from "belief" to "data" is illustrative of the type of ontological work that is performed upon Blackness in order to make the human real and social arrangements within the western context function. Data becomes the undisputed truth that permanently situates pejorative blackness to flexible fixated points of reference that allow the human to prosper. Data as a signifier of the sacred/material adherence makes pejorative blackness the only thing that it can be—depraved otherness.

It is the hollow edifice which science can fill with reactionary postulations of truth making that summon the tapestry of the human. Positioned as the supposition of the belief in false idols, the human via science as buttressed by data is fueled by the imposition of a most vile rendering of blackness. Thus, legibility is dependent upon pejorative blackness as a means to keep afloat the mythmaking processes inherent within the human project. Any rendering of blackness outside of the construction of the pejorative is not tenable. The proverbial center of state structures cannot hold the weight of Blackness outside of a pejorative positionality. Insecure in its position as the generator and curator of a debased and volatile hierarchical tradition, the churning of data and resultant theory reifies violence upon Blackness to protect the unstable nature of racial capitalism. Yet within the realm of the illegibility, Blackness exposes the fragility of the human project and as a direct result the many points of weakness within racial capitalism as a mythical construct. Rather than clamor for an impossible recognition as a legible subject, the genealogical impulse of Black collective movement and action has been to preserve the autonomous nature of Black knowledge traditions.

2

Police and the
Carceral Archival Project

The following archival document comes from the Coalition Against Police Abuse collection. The Coalition Against Police Abuse was founded as a collective in 1974 in response to the communal demand for an end to the processes that facilitated violence to Black people in Southern California at the hands of the police. Funded in part by the judgment won against the Pasadena Police Department for their attack upon collective member Michael Zinzun in which he lost an eye, CAPA had a very particular orientation toward police violence. On one hand, CAPA was clear that police violence was the manifestation of the state in its attempt to dampen dissent, revolt, and the adoption of Black ontological practices among the masses. Ranging from housing rights to state-facilitated environmental degradation, CAPA's aim of study was the multifaceted nature of the carceral state. On the other hand, CAPA firmly asserted that theory for social change had to be developed and synthesized from a Black episteme that foregrounded the masses of disenfranchised and dispossessed Black people around the globe. Situated together, a liberatory practice revealed the sophistication of Black liberation movements in tension with the overwhelming desire of the carceral state to suppress Blackness.

Militarism and Policing

In 1970, the Aerospace Corporation, commissioned by the City of Los Angeles, submitted an assessment plan entitled "Evaluation of the Proposed Tactical Information Correlation and Retrieval System." While a well-known entity within the world of military strategic development and technical systems building, the Aerospace Corporation was not (and is still not) as readily identifiable as the major players in the field such as Raytheon Technologies, Boeing, or Lockheed Martin Corporation. The Aerospace Corporation, formerly housed under the auspices of the United States Air Force, was established as a nonprofit organization in 1960 with virtually all of its funding derived from various tentacles within the Department of Defense. Established as the scientific wing of the US Air Force, the Aerospace Corporation was charged with the development and enhancement of military ballistic systems. As a nonprofit corporation, the Aerospace Corporation became the *de facto* conduit between the military, state, and local police agencies in the technological development of police infrastructures, intensifying their capabilities to repress potential threats to racial capitalist ordering systems.

The 1970 report detailed the intimate connection that the official bureaucratic mechanism of the US state project had made between the US military and the police. While there are clear limitations and differences between the two entities, such distinctions are those developed via the nation for matters of governance. Ideologically and materially, there is very little distinction between the two structures as they both function as emissaries of US nation-building and destabilization of epistemologies that are immersed within life-affirming traditions.

Rather than being abstract in nature, the relationship between the Aerospace Corporation and its affiliates such as the Los Angeles Police Department is one example in a long synergistic tradition of knowledge production emanating between the United States military and police agencies in the United States and around the world.

A small section of the report entitled "Law Enforcement Data Processing Applications" states:

> The applications of Electronic Data Processing (EDP) equipment to law enforcement areas may be divided into four groups: (1) sociological—the causes of crime and civil disorders, (2) operations—responding to crime events, riot control and crime deterrence, (3) investigative—solving specific crimes, and (4) analytic—analysis of criminal activity to support management decision-making on the tactical and strategic use of police resources. (Aerospace Corporation 1970, 13)

It is within this section that the intent and function of newly developed police technologies (via research conducted within the military) becomes apparent. The "causes of crime" is at its core a highly subjective metric/postulation/determination that masquerades as objective fact. It is important to note that crime as a sociological occurrence is a fictive racialized prop of modern humanism. The dossiers of the founding fathers of sociology and criminology alike are littered with violent racial treatises and diatribes against Black people to codify pejorative blackness as a normative fact of existence. Positioned as scientific fact and shielded by the perverse logics of research and data collection, these theories, which came to be the dominant expression of western empiricism, were the foundation of contemporary understandings of crime and civil disorder. Thus, crime and civil disorders, inventions of the state, are critical to understanding the insecurities of western intellectual thought.

Crime and the Human

The invention of crime and civil disorder as a matter of sociological fact has to be understood within its proper ideological and material context. The positioning of these fields of study / social facts / normative standards of lived conditions into their context provides a means to understand the precarity of western epistemological traditions via the human project. The construction of crime and civil disorder emanates from a philosophical tradition that is predicated and continues to thrive upon violent dispossession of knowledge production, material resources, and life. The ironic projection of crime and civil disorder onto Blackness can only be understood within the realm of the absurd, and yet it is one of the primary capacities of rational thought within the western intellectual tradition. Thus, the question has to be asked: What are crime and civil disorder?

Crime and civil disorder allow the state to maintain violent exploitation and simultaneously erase knowledge traditions that prove the fallacy of the human project, thus exposing the myth of western civilization as a totalizing enterprise. On the first account, crime and civil disorder situate the state as the ultimate benefactor undergirded by a set of moral principles informed by notions of individual liberty. As a result, any movement within the framework demands a reflexive internalization of the civil subject in contradistinction to the criminal. The criminal is the foil to proper engagement with the state apparatus. Even the most seemingly benign, liberal-based rhetorical inflections of the criminal reaffirm the unassailable position of the state: Youth need to be understood as students (and thus citizens in training); they are not criminals. Immigrants should be situated as hard working; they are not criminals. Nonviolent protesters are model citizens; they are not criminals. The framing of the criminal/civil subject in binary terms prevents the revelation of the much more insidious processes of racial capitalism. Lost within the fervent desire to label people and actions as criminal or deviant is the heinous multifaceted violence that is at the heart of the racial capitalist projects.

Within this paradigm, the invention of crime and civil disorder makes illegible epistemological traditions that refute western civilization as the normative standard of social arrangements and intellectual traditions. Rather than abide by a set of conditions that uphold the logics of the epistemological violence, Black epitomes reject western-informed militarism/carceral/domestic warfare frameworks and practices as a valid modality of life. Such a position leaves the state with very little room to maneuver other than through means of violent repression.

It is through the second aspect of "operations—responding to crime events, riot control and crime deterrence" that the conduit of violent repression is achieved. Once the establishment of crime and civil disorder has been determined a social fact, the state will go to all lengths to protect itself. Responding to crime events and riot control follows a genealogical path that has justified the brutal extraction and genocidal acts at the hands of western civilized despots under the guise of democratic values. Quite simply, it is the heavy hand of the state that is responsible for the most arduous tasks of imperial labor.

In juxtaposition to the iron fist, crime deterrence is the silent, innocuous component of state terror that is most reactionary in nature. Crime deterrence is informed by that fervent expression of the human project that is governed by notions of technological ingenuity and development. Utilizing the most advanced schema of repression, crime deterrence as a tool is boundless in its methodologies of terror to make illegible, neutralize and erase all perceived threats prior to their animation as a problem to the state. It should not come by any surprise that the nadir of predicative policing technologies was developed in the midst of vast uncertainty within a racial capitalist model that was teetering on the brink of exposure. Older technologies associated with crime repression, from organizational infiltration to various forms of audio surveillance, were called into question as a legitimate endeavor for a democratic process that juxtaposed itself against the supposed draconian nature of non-capitalist societies. Thus, the state in a moment of insecurity became even more repressive via clandestine means. Counter to the logic of transparency that was espoused as the mythical norm of justice within the civil project, the police as a structural apparatus increased violent repression through increased secrecy via new technologies. Hiding behind the burgeoning computer infrastructure, policing methodologies and practices were cloaked through coding schemes and racially based algorithms. Marketed as a social good under the auspices of efficiency and safety, the shift represented a reactionary pivot to a hyper focus on the elimination of the knowledge productions that disavowed the hierarchal formations inherent within the human project.

Carceral Reforms and the Archive

Points 3 and 4 of the Aerospace Corporation report (investigation and analysis) should be understood in tandem, as they are representative of the mythical system of justice that protects the freedom of the citizenry. Within the context of militarism as the normative structure of governance, the military and police were situated within categories that were superfluous to any rendering of individual liberty. There were no checks and balances upon a structural apparatus that was given the task of protecting the ideological tenets of racial capitalism.

The carceral archival project indicates that when agents of structural forces are "caught" in a nefarious position, they are brought to justice in accordance with the terms of western epistemological traditions. That is to say they are granted an expansive base of power within the system that not only vindicates their role and thereby the nation, but also provides the condition to further strengthen the structural capacity of the police to better protect the core tenets of racial capitalism. These points will be discussed further in chapter 3 as the role of science and, by extension, technology is critical to the capacity of the investigative and analytic capabilities of the police.

Given the intimate connection between policing and the military via warcraft as state policy, the liberal analysis of policing (and the carceral apparatus in general) as a provincial paradigm—focused on matters of civil rights and foreclosed opportunities related to individualized notions of social, political, and economic mobility—is shortsighted and functions to reproduce violence upon Black communities. Within such a liberal framework, great impetus has been placed upon legal challenges and limited reforms that will swing the scales of justice back to the center to provide "equal opportunity" for all citizens and those who strive to be citizens. Wrapped within an ideological conundrum that somehow the state will undo itself, the notion of police reform within the current epoch of the carceral archive project is one of the more absurd claims that consistently proves itself as faulty/foolish logic.

Yet the absurdity is not without precedent. The annals of social upheaval and radical action are littered with reactionary state posturing under the name of reform as means to (re)assert state authority and legitimacy. Through such practices we understand reform (specifically carceral reform) as a site of knowledge production and thus archival in formation and reproduction. Reforms are steeped within the violence-making capacity of ideological parameters that require Black subjugation. Rather than seek to fundamentally address the root cause of violence, carceral reforms by nature seek to preserve the most insidious aspects of said violence—state structures. The invocation (and maintenance) of the state structure provides an avenue for the incorporation of liberal-facing provocateurs into the state project to render its legitimacy to the masses. Clothed only in the robe of the civil (such as electoral politics), the liberal-inflected reform framework is devoid of the mechanizations that fuel the logics of racial capitalism and is thus woefully insufficient.

Such barren tactics provide a means by which reforms function as the conduit for state structures to become increasingly reactionary and thus more emboldened to enact truly heinous formations of violence. While the cooption of radical action through liberal reform schemes provides a veneer of "progress," the fascist intent of the carceral state intensifies under the banner of law and order. The law-and-order ethos coalesces around the tensions inherent within racial capitalism as means to transfer the ideological weight of said tensions upon Black ontological practices. Equipped with very little other than civil posturing, carceral reforms function as an anticipatory placation of the Black radical thought that situates the carceral state as a purveyor of multifaceted genocidal degradation. Thus, the severe limitations of the civil strategy are revealed through the limitations of state structures that are designed to uphold the legitimacy of the carceral enterprise.

Expressed as beneficent state projects, carceral reforms are archival in that they retain and deploy power to reify western ontological traditions. In this manner, reforms buttress the mythical conceit of the human through an erasure of Black ontologies that detail the violent exploitative impulses of carceral logics. Critically positioned as the corrective to unintended civic-based actions, carceral reforms are also archival in that they work to feed legitimacy back to state structures. During times of radical action, the archival component of carceral reforms is vital to state recuperation as it functions to make state structures appear normal.

Policing and War Making

Another critical dimension to the archival capacity of carceral reforms is the redirection of upheaval back to the civic and thus within the confines of the nation-state. Masking the geopolitical realities of racial capitalism, carceral reforms situate national imaginaries of a mythical past as the forecasting of a supposed utopic future. The effect of this archival schema is the distortion of the intimate relationship among carceral capacities across geopolitical spheres. Momentarily setting aside the circus that is carceral reform, of great concern is the manner that policing has been separated from the inherent violence of racial capitalism. The function of the police has been branded as a matter of protection—protection of the safety and well-being of citizens within the state apparatus. The function of policing is indeed about protection but has very little to do with mythical constructs of individualized notions of safety; rather it is about the protection of the critical mechanisms and inner workings of racial capitalism. Policing functions to shield the ideological, theoretical, and philosophical traditions within western epistemology that demand vapid exploitation of people, land, and knowledge production based upon a violent imposition of hierarchies. It is within such a framework that we can understand policing, and thus the carceral archival project, as not being bounded by the nation. Instead, policing works within a multifaceted network of structures that extend beyond the constructions of national borders.

One of the primary partners/extensions of policing during late capitalism has been the military. Symbolic of a reactionary posturing that has been marked by the devolving of western imperialism during late capitalism, the bolstering of the military has been a primary mechanism to maintain hierarchies that are central to racial capitalist endeavors. War making was not relegated solely to occupation and destabilization outside national boundaries, but within them as well. The United States developed an internal social infrastructure that was predicated upon the logics of war. Rather than being hyperbolic in nature, the intimate connection between the military and the police is evident in the carceral archives which document the intricate details of how war-making technologies that had been developed within the Department of War (later renamed the Department of Defense) were passed on to matters of domestic warcraft—policing.

Facilitated by bureaucratic state actions such as grants and the formation of agencies and task forces, police did not simply become militarized in terms of weaponry—the police are part and parcel of a drastically bloated and emboldened defense apparatus. To this end, police worked in tandem with the military to prevent dissent/revolt/reimagining. The carceral archival project also details the development of technological schema utilized by the military and police, working in tandem, at the behest of racial capitalist interest to eliminate, make illegible, and violently subjugate labor collectives, radical organizing, and knowledge traditions that presented models of social relationships not immersed in the violence hierarchies.

The function of policing has to be understood within the context of its material and ideological relationship to the core tenets of racial capitalism—brutal forms of exploitation based upon the difference-making projects that (re)produce hierarchies. Policing in this context is immersed within defense strategies based upon war methodologies and tactics. As a result, there is a natural amalgamation between the military and the police as their core mission is to defend the madness unleashed by western civilization. The logics of such a relationship extend beyond the borders of the nation in part to protect the fictive schema of national borders as a social fact. Perhaps more important, the reactionary dynamics of the relationship reveal the insecure and untenable position of western epistemological traditions that have attempted to legitimize the human project as the normative basis of social relationships.

3

Technology and
the Social Sciences
as Synergistic Violence

From the advent of word processors and personal computers to the prevalence of social media as one of the dominant modalities of communication, the commonsense framing of computational technology has been focused on the individual (consumer) engagement with computing systems. Yet from virtually the moment that computational technology was developed, it has been a central tool for various state archival projects and thus vital to the enforcement of the boundary-making and violence-inducing capacity of the state. The current iteration of state governance via carceral management has been well documented and historicized by scholars and researchers of police and policing who have meticulously parsed the manner in which specific technological advancements and data collection schemes have been critical to the refinement and enhancement of the carceral project. Centering the analysis from the LA BPP and CAPA collections, this chapter offers a meditation upon distillation of study as a critical component of planning and organizing.

While the origins and mission of CAPA were discussed in the previous chapter, the Los Angeles chapter of the Black Panther

Party was a foundational component of the radical organizing against the carceral state that developed during the late 1960s and early 1970s. Placing great emphasis on the multiplicity of the carceral state apparatus, the LA BPP's analysis revealed the carceral state to be greatly influenced by the militaristic aims of the US imperial designs of global domination and terror. To this end, the LA BPP was particularly attuned to the various technologies and ideologies of control that were centered on counterrevolutionary tactics as developed by the carceral state. Informed by an unrelenting love for the Black community, the analysis of carcerality was directly indebted to an analysis of the state that was derived from the Black communal experience.

A cursory synopsis of the CAPA and LA BPP collection reveals that organizers were highly attuned to the technological mechanizations that were being levied against them and utilized every resource at their disposal to study the core aspects of such systems and their linkages across time and space. Such awareness was broadcast loudly throughout Black neighborhoods and became the harbinger for future endeavors of an insatiable carceral apparatus. Very simply, the technological advances of the 1960s and '70s that have spawned an array of surveillance techniques (satellite systems and tracking devices) and amalgamation stratagems among computing devices (data collection systems such as PredPol/Geolitica) were studied, fought against, and forecasted as having a deleterious impact upon Black liberatory movements across the globe.* The following is an effort to resituate the gen-

---

* PredPol was established through a partnership between professors from the University of California, Los Angeles, and the Los Angeles Police Department. Spearheaded by cofounder and professor of anthropology Jeff Brantingham, a core mission of PredPol was to use data analytics to predict where crime was going to take place in order to direct the LAPD to where they should direct the bulk of their militaristic resources—hence the shorthand for the name, predictive policing = PredPol. Building an expansive network through academic channels throughout California and subsequently across the country, the research

esis of such thinking from Black radical collectives and Black intellectual thought.

The Perils of Data

In 1965 the California Criminal Justice Information System (CC-JIS) was established via a grant awarded by the Law Enforcement Assistance Administration in conjunction with a budget allocation from the California Assembly. CCJIS was designed to transform the manner in which records of activity deemed to be criminal were inputted, collected, stored, accessed, and utilized. In shifting away from a data collection system that was described as "incomplete" and "inaccurate," a primary goal was the development of a central database that could be accessed by policing agencies, court systems, and agents of the criminal justice system throughout the state. By 1972 the project had been deemed a success, and in a report to the Joint Legislative Audit Committee of the California Assembly, the State of California looked to expand the system with the allocation of an increased budget.

Located in the middle of the report was a seemingly relatively minor point that was quickly picked up by community organizers who began waving the proverbial red flag and cautioned against the design and implementation of this massive system. The report states:

> One of the factors used in developing the criteria for determining what data is to be considered CJIS cognizant is

---

from PredPol was (and continues to be) the basis of countless research articles, grant awards, nonprofit partnerships, and conference presentations. From this research, entities such as the LAPD and other law enforcement agencies began to impose intense forms of hypersurveillance and violence upon Black communities, as Black communities were deemed areas at risk of crime. In the aftermath of much pushback from Black communal organizations, PredPol has recently changed its name to Geolitica.

cost benefit. There are many types of non serious offenses which are considered to be CJIS non cognizant because the cost of converting and maintaining the data in the automated file is considered to be greater than is warranted for the benefits derived. There are, however, a significant number of records being included in the automated file where the offense does not seem to warrant the cost. Many of these records consist of only one offense, which was either not prosecuted or was dismissed in court. Most of these records are related to drug arrests. Data of this type does not appear to be the kind of criminal history information which would justify the expenditure necessary for inclusion in an automated file, the prime purpose of which is the prompt identification of serious criminal offenders. (Joint Legislative Audit Committee 1972, 3)

Organizations such as the Black Panther Party and later the Coalition Against Police Abuse followed a very trusted mantra that if the state built it, it was going to be used to its furthest extent. In this case, while the records indicated that such a database was going to be utilized only for "serious offenders," organizers were fully aware that it did not take much to change the meaning of categories of "serious" versus "non serious." The insight and knowledge of community organizers was spot on, as within ten years the definition of serious crime had dramatically changed. The 1980s ushered in the draconian "War on Drugs" campaign and the very database system that organizers had warned about less than ten years prior was the same hub used to deploy a wide array of military assault weaponry against Black communities under the guise of curbing the drug war. Perhaps the most pernicious of these weapons was the infamous battering ram, a fourteen-foot armored tank accompanied by a team of SWAT officers armed in high-grade military gear. These tactical units would be deployed to "drug" locations archived within the database network established by CCJIS. Civil rights organizations raised concerns, as very often mothers and children who were sound asleep would be violently awoken by the dismantling of their houses as a giant tank ripped through walls and entryways. A multifaceted violent system, the state, through technological archiving projects, had mapped war onto Black communities, and Black subjects were the targets.

Science, Technology, and Ontological Violence

The utilization of science within western epistemological traditions has largely been based upon the production of concepts/ frameworks that reify the violent logics of the human project. The myth of science within the linear narrative of western historical convention has been to position rational thinking, and thus science, under the auspices of an advanced civilization. The rendering of the linear progression from the divine to the scientific is illustrative of this convention. Buttressed by continued myth building, science has become one of the heralded achievements of the human project. At the core of this myth is the notion that science, through the continued advent of technological advancements, has produced a more refined and polished modality of thought. Within this paradigm, scientific precepts are virtually unassailable. Further, technology, a central component of myth-making, has been constructed as the machinery that moves civilization toward grander heights. Yet the archives of western thought reveal a much more insidious function of science and the manner in which technology as a lever of modern humanism has been instrumental in the maintenance of repressive hierarchies.

A core aspect of technology within the human project has been the development of multifaceted weaponry that has no other recourse outside of the meting out of sheer, brutal violence. The archive of plantation records throughout the modern era demonstrates the sickening imaginative capacity of western epistemological traditions to develop heinous weapons/contraptions/devices that were designed for the purpose of inflicting multiple forms of terror upon Black populations. For the purpose of labor suppression and the suppression of freedom, the scope and type of violence-making mechanisms knew no bounds. Perhaps the most curious aspect of this tradition was that death was not always the purpose or intent of these technological advancements. Rather, one of the key goals was to inflict the mythical conceptualizations of hell upon the lives of Black people, creating a state of permanent purgatory.

The framing of history as a linear narrative provides an easy escape hatch to forgive, forget, or erase the technological advancements of the modern era. That the sins of the father should not burden his children is a mantra culturally codified into the precepts of western epistemological traditions. As a result, the intimate connection between technology and overt fronts of brutal violence at the root of the contemporary carceral apparatus has been erased. Given that the origins of carcerality were imbricated in some of the most infamous technological experiments/disasters/developments within western civilization, it should not come as a surprise that science as a platform to test the upper registers of human pain/existence/trauma has been a key informant in the contemporary carceral apparatus.

The development of high-capacity death machines in conjunction with weaponry that possessed the capability to precisely target the most sensitive regions of the human body via advanced technological ingenuity was a hallmark of the contemporary carceral period. Yet, just as important was the development of systems/machines/mechanisms/procedures that were intended to test the outer limits of human existence. Given that Black people have been rendered as illegible subjects, the human project was given carte blanche to utilize the unlimited scope of the state resource trove and unleash the gross methodologies of the western science tradition upon Black people. This provided for the means to suppress knowledge production within Black communities the world over, but also provided for fertile testing grounds. That is to say, technological developments within the contemporary carceral era are key components of the human project, and as a project it is constantly testing capacities of terror to maintain hierarchies.

Technology and Archival Capacity

Utilizing the schema that was the underlay of the California Criminal Justice Information System, the centrality of technology to the carceral archive project is revealed. In a very rudimentary archival formulation, the purpose and intent of the CCJIS was to gather and collect information on a population that was understood as an existential threat to the logics of racial capitalism. However, the primary function of CCJIS was much more than just data collection, as it was the primer that legitimated the analytic association of Blackness with the noncivil. The formations of reasoning as a rational element of human thought were articulated through technical instruments such as the CCJIS throughout the modern carceral period. Granted the power of supreme moral and ethical authority (through specious claims of objectivity), CCJIS was able to circumvent the demands of radical transparency that were central to Black radical organizing. While seemingly a minor point within the grand scheme of state surveillance and terror, it is of note that during the 1970s and 1980s the demands of anticarceral organizing, without fail, led with the need for the state to have complete transparency with relation to the burgeoning carceral technology infrastructure.

Once the foundation of the moral authority and reasoning was violently substantiated as a claim to legitimacy, the archival underpinnings of the technological advancements bled into virtually every aspect of state governance. Informed by the logics of rampant, hyperaggressive nontransparent data collection mechanisms, these archival streams were then connected and utilized to inflict multiple forms of violence upon the very Black populations who had warned about the draconian intentions of the carceral technological sphere. Perhaps the most grotesque ironic juxtaposition of this process was the way the state utilized extremely violent means under the guise of public safety as a means to maintain insecure living conditions for Black communities. Ranging from intentional abandonment and removal of critical resources such as food, shelter, and access to health resources to gross forms of material and ideological enclosure, the legitimization of such acts was made legible through the archival capacity of the carceral technological sphere. Such capacity reveals the encompassing nature of the technical apparatus as it both produces human and nonhuman subjects and through such production justifies the existence of the nonhuman as evidence within the parameters of the mechanization that facilitated the production. Anecdotally, CCJIS not only creates nonhuman Black subjectivity, but once ensnared within the inner workings of such a technological structure, the output (loss of housing, resources, health care) is justification and evidence for the nonhuman positionality thrust upon Black people.

The core tenets of the technology that informed the massive killing and suppression apparatus of this period were initially hypotheses and postulations that were based upon the theoretical considerations associated with pejorative blackness. Akin to any good hypothesis, such ideas had to be tested as a measure of violent suppression and relatedly, the techniques had to be understood within the context of lived environments.

Once tested in the field, the studies were repeatedly replicated in Black communities throughout the world. The state functioning as the bureaucratic apparatus provided the means through which these technologies would be imported to cities, states, and other nations. Through means of government facilitation, which took a variety of forms ranging from grant competitions to diplomatic missions, these processes became the normative standard under which Black communal existence was situated.

The result of the technological experimentation/innovation/development during the contemporary carceral era was the transformation of Black communities into sites under permanent siege and terror. Through the utilization and perfection of sophisticated killing and life-altering technology, western imperialism attempted to corral and make superfluous Black life. Akin to the testing and employment of technology during the plantation era, the methodological consideration of the lived conditions presented within late capitalism as a distinct epoch was a key aspect to the development of the weaponry systems. Given the sprawl of Black people and communities in various living conditions, the modeling of technological innovations was very much a site-specific enterprise. While there were general forms of technological advancements that were utilized throughout the world, one of the key shifts during the carceral period was a specialization of warcraft technology for very specific regions. As a result, the deployment of material resources became attuned to the demands of geographic regions, and the sharing of information very much became an enterprise based upon conditions of life: various forms of urbanism, rural communities, and extreme climate-based conditions.

The grouping of regions based upon technological development had a profound impact upon the construction of pejorative blackness in the carceral era. Black people became identifiable through the type of criminal behavior that justified the particular type of technological control / death mechanisms that were utilized upon them. Functioning in the typical dual processor scope of western suppression techniques, the technologies of control not only justified their own existence but also functioned as a tool to erase Black knowledge customs and practices. In this manner the scientific development that came to represent the carceral era was emblematic of the reactionary nature of western epistemological schema. Blackness had to be transformed from its internationalist, multisited organizing-based tactics of movement building and life-affirming strategies to a geographic specific bastion of concocted evil. To establish pejorative blackness during late capitalism, it was imperative for technological innovation and deployment to reinforce the hierarchical differences that were central to the human project. The technologies of death/terror/suppression of the carceral era reinforced borders in direct response to the knowledge and communal traditions of Black people that identified the dismantling/transcendence/disregard of borders as a key site of material, intellectual, and cultural struggle.

The result was a multifaceted military-police infrastructure that utilized all the resources at the state's disposal to enforce the perverse logics of a one-dimensional caricature denoted through pejorative blackness. In tandem with the technological advancements of the propaganda machine of the nation apparatus, the nation spent unseemly resources to destroy/contain/transform Black communal spaces under the rubric of western epistemological traditions. Geographically specific forms of pejorative blackness were splayed across televisions, education textbooks, newspapers, radio waves, and a myriad of other public consumptive formats as a means to indoctrinate the general public to its associated technological apparatus as a normative condition of life. Technologies of extreme violence that were initially habituated and tested upon Black communities during moments of "extreme upheaval" were now employed as a daily manifestation of Black life—and the vast propaganda capacity of western imperialism was there to document and reproduce a narrative of the necessity of such technologies.

Counterintelligence, Science, and the Archival

As learned from the defeats during previous eras, Black communal logics and knowledge productions were far too sophisticated to be undermined through brute force. A critical aspect of the police infrastructure during the carceral era was the utilization of counterintelligence measures that had three basic functions: archiving, disrupting, and authority building. As had been the case during previous epochs' utilization of counterintelligence tactics, western scientific advances were critical to the employment of counterintelligence design and implementation during the carceral era.

Archiving was perhaps the most important component measure to the development of counterintelligence schemes within late capitalism. The essential framing of scientific models and modes of inquiry was situated around the enhancement of the efficiency, scope, and stealth of archive-based mechanisms. It was during this period that western states infused substantial resources into the development of covert systems that would be the basis of carceral archiving. Both ideologically and materially, racialized terror and warcraft through militarism became the dominant mode of cultural and intellectual expression of late capitalism within the western nation-state. Spreading through all forms of structural life in the state apparatus, unabated allegiance to militarism (and by extension the burgeoning carceral project) became the normative adherence to state identification. Thus, virtually all forms of state life including, most prominently, labor and education came to produce and reproduce the western project of the human via militarism. This seepage into multiple forms of state life was vital for the establishment of covert technologies that would be utilized for the development of massive archiving networks.

It is important to note that while the effect of militarism had always been a central component to western imperialism, the effect of labor and community organizing leading up to the carceral era had generated an outward distrust of formal and informal tenets of state structures in daily life. The expansion of the military into these sectors had the effect of suppressing the basis of these labor and organizing relationships while also normalizing the presence of militarism as a social benefit. The development of covert archiving technologies that would be key components of Black suppression and thus the legibility of pejorative blackness could only be achieved with the massive shift of militarism into state life.

The result of this shift was the proliferation of covert technological mechanisms that provided the policing infrastructure with new machinery ranging from high-speed portable data collection capability to advanced surveillance systems that could pinpoint exact location. With no further need to develop such systems under the secrecy of classified state projects, the expansion of militarism into state life provided the ideological (and material) means for such technological developments to be undertaken in the normative structurization of education and labor. Once underway, the vast network established by the state began to undertake the other key components of covert technological capacity: disruption and authority building.

The disruptive and authority-building aspects of the covert technological apparatus were tandem-capacity-building instruments that facilitated the attempted removal and terror-inflicted destabilization of Black life. On the authority-building front, the basis of the technology was established in accordance with state structures that sought to reify pejorative blackness. The state utilized the vast collection of carceral-based archival data and methodologies to establish a type of crude legitimacy within the teetering social arrangements established within the late capitalism human project. The legitimization efforts were most readily seen within the vast networks established within systems of jurisprudence and academia. The codification of pejorative blackness through law, policy, and social custom based on covert technology data collection and mining was central to the nation's attempt to shore up the gaping fissures that were present within the hierarchal arrangements. The result of these dynamics led to the facilitation of Black people to sites of captivity and extreme violence. The buildup of the carceral system was marked by a vast array of forms of containment. The relationship with the structures of justice created an infinity loop whereby the structures of justice were fed an insatiable amount of data via the covert technological apparatuses used to destabilize Black life. The carceral technologies that were employed to enact the destabilization of Black life were fattened through the means of jurisprudence and consequently demanded more from these structures, which in turn led to the inflation of structures of jurisprudence. In metropoles, suburban outliers, and rural communities, the intimate relationship between covert technologies and systems of justice became the normative barometer of life. The destabilization, destruction, and containment of Black life was and continues to be the basis by which civil society functions. Specifically, the extraction of capital from the disruption of Blackness forms the basis by which civil society provides allocation of material resources to legible subjects, a key factor in the maintenance of hierarchies.

The Academy, Blackness, and the Human

While the justice structures worked to facilitate the material extraction of Black life, the academic enterprise quickly acquiesced to the vilification required to make pejorative blackness real. Via state funding mechanisms (through both formal and privately funded channels), research programs, curricular development, and formal government partnerships, the academic landscape, most notably within the biological and social sciences and the humanities, developed theories and ideological paradigms that located blackness as a scourge that was void of culture (outside of nihilistic tropes) and whose presence within the scope of civil society was a violent, menacing presence that needed to be contained and removed.

The imperial designs of western statecraft provided the schema by which the academic enterprise became the lifeblood of carceral epistemological endeavors. Such an imperial logic lays bare the crucial archival role of the academy within the development and maintenance of the carceral epoch. Specifically, the burgeoning cold war military expansion of US statecraft throughout the world was the material ground upon which academia was a critical partner in the disruption, unsettling/settling, and puppeteering of communities around the globe. While the infamous examples of nefarious academic projects such as Project Camelot conducted throughout South America and the myriad invasive research experiments conducted in Southeast Asia in the lead-up to and during the Vietnam War are often cast as outliers and/or hidden, the methodological and theoretical directives developed during these endeavors were central to the development of disciplinary training and epistemological enhancement. Within the purview of imperial conquest, as informed by Project Camelot and anthropological endeavors in Southeast Asia, the archival function of the academy has to be understood as a repository for the storage and enhanced reimplementation of violence-making processes in one region to be deployed in another. Quite simply, the lines of continuity between Project Camelot, the Vietnam War, and predicative policing technologies used in Los Angeles are threaded together via the western academic enterprise. The development of distinct methodological practices and research endeavors is funded, tested, and refined in regions throughout the world to support specific forms of warcraft against populations who are deemed to be hostile to demands of exploitation and suffering. In the case of the carceral archive, a symbiotic relationship emerged whereby academic technologies, theories, and methodologies developed outside the United States became critical to suppression of the Black liberation efforts within the United States. Similarly, as documented in the life of Black Panther Party member Geronimo Ji Jaga, who was held in violent captivity for over twenty years and tortured via means of psychological warfare developed within the western academy, carceral spaces in the United States became key sites of academic experimentation and warcraft that were then exported in efforts to fulfil racial capital imperial fantasies in key sites across the globe.

While brutal regimes of violent suppression were/are critical to western imperialism and warcraft, a central task of academia and the social sciences in particular was (and continues to be) to provide the veneer of civility that legitimates and obscures the violence of the carceral state. The primary means by which this was achieved was through the advancing of theoretical premises that frame and situate Blackness as different—and such difference was cast within a binary mold as fundamentally abhorrent in relation to constructed non-Black (and thereby human) subjects. From medical postulations that rendered Blackness as crazed and/or permanently askew to social theory claims that positioned Black life, culture, and social visions as incongruent with civil society, the full scope of these theoretical assertions legitimated the containment, exploitation, and suppression of Blackness.

Following in the tradition of the human project, the western academic tradition employed the covert technological innovations to provide the justification for hierarchies as the basis of social relationships. The academic wing of the human project developed the theoretical platforms and frameworks that demanded the enactment of policing as a means to suppress Black life. Working in tandem with land speculators, technocrats, and finance capitalists, the academic wing provided the rationale for the removal of Black people from their communities as a means to develop new schemes of capital extraction. Emboldened by covert technologies that were developed in concert with the academic tradition, "scholars" used the data to develop pseudo-intellectual frameworks that created a new type of pejorative blackness to fit the needs of the carceral era. Once this paradigm was established and reproduced, the results demanded the removal of Black people through the logistics of the carceral network.

Yet, while the social sciences were central to the development of theoretical platforms that undergirded the need to develop, refine, and deploy material technologies of racialized and gendered violence, a central aspect of the academic enterprise was the degradation and disarticulation of the soul from the Black nonhuman subject. Functioning as a laboratory on a grand scale, academic disciplines writ large, and the social sciences specifically, were designed with the explicit intentions of chiseling away Blackness from western ontological practices. Cohering a vast archival project, the hallways, classrooms, basements, attics, libraries, museums, and warehouses on university, college, and primary and secondary school campuses were and continue to be repositories of a vast array of sordid technological and ideological schemes that cohered imperial projects.

While the carceral epoch has been marked by a vast siphoning of social, political, and economic resources to the military/police nexus, academia has been instrumental in both establishing pernicious myths and perfecting technologies of containment and violence. The mythmaking apparatus focused on the production of black waywardness while simultaneously (and in tandem with) reifying economic and political responsibilities to the individual. Situating these myths within a fictive past, the archival capacity of academia fashioned social arrangements into a technological hellscape (in the name of social advancement through linear tropes) that continues to be governed by the very logics that make carceral governance appear rational. The intent of these myths has been to mask the array of scientific and humanistic experimental processes that developed the ideological and technological expertise critical to the maintenance of the carceral epoch. Informed by the ontological violence inherent within the foundation of academia, the management and distribution of carceral suppression was a key feature of academic enterprise.

From the perspective of the human project, science and the proliferation of various technological substrata are vital to both undermining and making Black knowledge traditions. The organizational structure of Black knowledge traditions and modalities of life demonstrated the multiplicity of ways of being, a paradigm that was antithetical to the binary framing of western hierarchies. Blackness was situated as an oppositional impossibility that had to be contained. Logics of Black life ranging from labor-organizing strategies to the most mundane aspects of daily Black life represented a threat to the western human project that demanded adherence to hierarchical norms. The western imagination was left to roam within the archive of epistemological traditions that had developed the most grotesque killing machines and life-suppressing technologies. The result was the continued unleashing of a violent imperialist madness upon the world in order to sustain ontological practices that attempted to keep racial capitalist logic afloat.

4
Environmental Instability

Southern California is often marketed and understood as a region dominated by lush beaches surrounded by picturesque mountain ranges. The weather is always perfect, and you will never be bothered by the inconvenience of extreme heat, cold, or moisture via humidity or rain and snow. Such a marketing plan belies a not so pleasant reality of the region: it is highly polluted (both air and ground) and given the consequences of overdevelopment and climate change is prime for rampant wildfires and frequent land shifting such as mudslides. Historically, the general calmness of the weather and the proximity to a stable coastline has made this region plum for the extraction of natural resources which can then be quickly dispersed throughout the world. One of the dominant forms of natural resource extraction throughout Southern California is oil and its subsequent refinement into various oil-based products. As well-documented within the litany of internal memos, founding documents, and journal articles found throughout several archival collections, there was an intense focus on the dynamics among the oil industry and the populations that were most affected by the encroachment of their extractive reach.

The archival records present a most interesting dichotomy with regard to "Big Oil" and the concerns of communities and various organizing efforts against fossil fuel–based energy extraction. The 1970s were a significant turning point in the conversation regarding energy consumption throughout the world. In part because of the Organization of the Petroleum Exporting Countries (OPEC) oil embargo that resulted in a severe oil shortage and long lines at gas stations, a general recognition arose that there was something off about an economic model that relied heavily upon a source of energy that was not readily accessible domestically and did not readily replenish itself. In addition to such concern, internal memos from energy companies such as Exxon revealed a serious anxiety about the move away from oil as the dominant energy form and the fact that the combination of conservation efforts and depletion of oil reserves throughout the world would result in a shifting energy extraction landscape.

While corporations such as Exxon developed strategies to ensure the stability of their profit margins, there was a growing schism within the United States between those who understood the 1970s moment as vital to the restructuring of energy consumption (and thus the environment) and the particular interest within the federal government, which sought to maintain a particular form of stasis with regard to the fossil fuel industry despite its readily apparent fragility as a resource.

Reflective of the severe limitations of racial capitalist endeavors, the fragility of violent resource extraction was emblematic of the imperial project itself. Within the collections of radical organizers, and specifically within the collections of the Coalition Against Police Abuse and the Los Angeles chapter of the Black Panther Party, there was an explicit connection made between the coloniality of oil extraction and its impact upon Black communities. Utilizing such a framework provided the lens to understand the material and ideological dynamics in Southern California as intimately connected to material and ideological dynamics in the Niger Delta. A central component that linked such imperial projects across the globe was the rise of militarism (and thus persistent warfare) as the dominant mode of governance. The warfare apparatus central to western ontological projects was vital to destruction of land and communities. Carcerality, understood as the logical application of militarism within the United States, was cojoined to matters of resource extraction and the multiscalar effects that resulted in Black communal dispossession. Following in line with the genealogical edicts of the human project, the response by the carceral state was to invoke the notion of the civil to both substantiate claims to land and normalize violent resource extraction while also attempting to make illegible / eradicate the social vision of Black radical organizers who were making plain the intentions of western imperialistic endeavors.

Environment, Political Economy, and Angst

One of the primary areas of concern raised by organizing collectives was the connection between extractive waste and the prevalence of cancer. Organizing efforts from around the country brought public health officials, scientists, workers, and community residents together to form a multifaceted campaign against the reliance upon fossil fuel–based extraction. On local levels, these efforts pushed for the transparency of private corporations and public utilities, demanding they release information on the dangers of chemicals involved in various extractive processes and, importantly, publicly state where such chemicals were dumped. The latter concern was of grave importance, as many Black communities had been built directly upon toxic waste sites where Black residents had no idea that their homes were sitting atop a toxic mine with potentially fatal consequences. At a national level, a slew of congressional bills put forward aimed to implement severe restrictions on oil companies via ordinances and fine structures that sought to curb the flagrant dumping of chemicals, a process that these companies had engaged in for over fifty years. While these efforts mostly focused on the public policy front, there were additional campaigns waged to close oil drilling and refining operations with a history of spewing toxic waste into the air as a by-product of the process.

These collective efforts and campaigns were met with a chilly response by the carceral apparatus that sought to maintain law and order during a momentous shift. In the wake of the 1970s crises, the Law Enforcement Assistance Administration within the United States Department of Justice formed an Emergency Energy Committee. The committee issued a report in 1974 simply entitled "Preliminary Report on Crime and the Energy Crisis." The report is a fascinating read into the manner in which the federal government, rather than pivot and begin a wide campaign to invest in alternative energy sources that would transition away from fossil fuels, looked to further its position in the extraction of nonrenewable energy. In other words, the report sought to double down on oil via the carceral apparatus.

The report was fairly blasé about the tremendous impact that the crises would have upon the day-to-day lives of laborers. The report states, "In some communities the unemployment problem has been even more severe because of the strong dependence of the economy of the particular community on energy-related products (e.g., automobile manufacturing, petrochemicals, recreation, and private aircraft)" (4). The report continues, "Some increases in the crime of shoplifting and other types of petty larceny may occur, but the most significant impact of this problem to law enforcement agencies will occur in the areas such as marital disputes, drinking-related problems, suicides, and other areas related to personal depression" (5).

While the report was fairly cold about the interpersonal impact upon workers, the government was very concerned about how such dissatisfaction would lead to workers' collective and massive uprisings. Castigating worker strikes as inherently violent and/or prone to violence, the report states:

> The second area of concern arises from the violent protests of groups of individuals affected by the energy shortage. The most significant example to date is the truckers' protests. Drawing national attention by truck blockades of highways in Ohio and Pennsylvania, the truckers' situation has deteriorated until there have been reports of numerous drivers being shot at in various states, drivers being assaulted, and rocks and bricks being dropped on windshields of trucks from overpasses as striking truckers attempted to discourage the operations of non-striking truckers. The National Guard has been utilized in several states to counter the widespread occurrences of such incidents by guarding highway overpasses to prevent objects from being dropped. Aerial patrols have been instituted over major highways in some states.
>
> Similar incidents could easily spread to other groups. Conceivably, violence can arise from strikes by impacted labor groups or by large groups of laid-off workers. In addition, citizens' groups may become actively engaged in protests or demonstrations which may lead to violence, particularly at retail gasoline or diesel fuel outlets. (LEAAEEC 1974, 3)

The report is full of anxieties directly related to "crimes" against the state including "larceny, theft and robbery," "falsification of records," "black markets," "bribery," "price violations," and a host of other "violent" and "white collar crime." Setting aside the absurd issue, as documented within the archival collection, that establishment of the fossil fuel energy infrastructure is predicated upon these various "crimes," the most prominent issue is that while laborers, organizers, public health officials, residents, and a host of other constituents were developing plans to move away from the violent multiscalar processes inherent within oil extraction, the state was making plans to utilize the crises as a way to increase its capacity to incarcerate individuals and to curtail dissent and protests.

Decolonization, Imperialism, and the Environment

Plumbing the archives of radical organizing against the carceral state revealed a common tendency: an insistent analysis of the environment writ large including energy extraction, natural resource exploitation, agricultural manipulation and labor suppression, multiple forms of toxicity, land displacement, and the constant specter of global warming. Given the consistent analysis of and organizing around the environment, the analytical, theoretical, and applied connections all pointed to the need for a rigorous engagement with the burgeoning carceral apparatus and its relationship to environmental destruction/manipulation/extraction. Informed by a decolonial orientation, the analysis rendered by these organizations pushed for an understanding of the nation as a complex formation that utilized various configurations of exploitation to coalesce interests among the many interlocutors of capital. Such orientation was most explicitly stated within the collections of the Coalition Against Police Abuse and the Los Angeles chapter of the Black Panther Party. The decolonial framework was of vital importance as struggles occurring throughout West Africa and Southeast Asia greatly informed the political analysis and subsequent strategy of both organizations. Within such a framework, the mapping of the environment as a primary site of study upon advanced forms of western imperial projects throughout the world was crucial to understanding the motivations of the carceral apparatus.

This revealed the intimate relationship between struggles for land and food and the fossil fuel industry. As such, oil conglomerates were positioned as a dire threat because of their violent practice of destroying the earth's vital resources as well as their compulsion to destroy the people and their corresponding ontological practices seeking to maintain and reproduce resources vital to the earth. The framing of the destruction of the environment as not merely a looming existential crisis that would occur sometime in the future but an immediate concern that wreaked havoc across intersecting geographies paved the ground to organize across multiple communities and spaces.

Further, decolonial praxis marked the military as a key articulation of racial capitalists' desire to exploit, consume, and suppress Black radical organizations. In that vein CAPA and the BPP understood that the militaristic function of nation-states was informed by corporate ideological foundations that demanded the removal of people from the land and from vital resources in the name of exploitation. In a concrete manner, environmental degradation was connected to land dispossession and its resultant food shortages and health calamities.

Applying the logic of colonial empire-building and expansion to the primary impulse of environmental degradation in the United States, the carceral apparatus was understood as the manifestation of domestic warfare. In ways similar to the formation of the state structures that dispossessed Black people of their land in colonial outposts throughout West Africa, US state structures played a vital role in facilitating the violent reallocation of land and the dispossession of Black people in the United States. Utilizing the full spectrum of the carceral apparatus, state authorities via civil networks established by the law and the (re)invention of criminality provided the legitimacy to target Black people for violent dispossession while also subjecting Black communities to life in environmentally degraded areas. Thus, the interstices between the environment and carcerality could be readily identified, organized against, and moved upon to open pathways toward liberation.

Militarism, Carcerality, and Resource Exploitation

The massive shift in the economic model of governance in the United States following World War II had profound implications for the dynamics of labor, land, and communities around the country. Most notably, as mentioned in the previous chapter, the growth of military Keynesianism laid bare the violent tendencies of an expansive military complex that aimed to contain/corral/destabilize Black life. The archives of Black radical organizing reveal the importance of understanding the development of the carceral state within the purview of expansive militarism. Developed within a multifaceted analytical understanding that the tentacles of capital exploitation were built upon a set of common interests, the mapping of the carceral state revealed a complex web of violent manipulation of communities, resources, and the built environment. The archives connected the often-hidden dots leading to the broader logics of racial capitalism, illuminating the multiple forms of violence inflicted upon Black communities. The hyperexploitation of natural resources had a direct impact upon western nation-building and attempts to maintain a violent hierarchical imbalance. In sum, the archives of radical organizers point to the curious multifaceted intimacy between resource extraction and empire-building, resulting in environmental and communal degradation and the massive development of the carceral infrastructure.

While oil had been a key target of western civilization expansion since the nineteenth century, the geopolitical dynamics of the post–World War II landscape revealed the precarity of western states' economic stability vis-à-vis a lack of control of oil production and manipulation. It was within this landscape that the United States inserted itself as a key figure within the future of racial capitalist relationships among nation-states. With an acute focus on the gross expansion of militarism as a strategy of political governance, the United States simultaneously staked its position as an outlier to market fluctuations resulting from the tensions between nonwestern oil-producing countries and a western consumer base while establishing itself as the proverbial strongman defending the interests of western civilization.

It was at these interstices that radical organizers developed a robust analysis which framed carcerality as part of a larger militaristic project seeking to destabilize long-held land relationships, thus framing carcerality beyond the limited scope of provincial governance and pushing the popular narrative of the environment as resting in the realm of individual responsibility.

The significance of developing a theoretical model that situated the environment within the context of multiple positionalities provided for a clear understanding of western imperialistic motivations. Within this framing, the study of the environment encompassed the grand narrative of violent expansion that utilized methodologies developed through scientific endeavors as well as the reification of the human through processes of labor, material, and land extraction. Thus, the organizing tendencies/imperatives of radical organizing removed the veil of the nation's intrusion into communities as a benevolent provider of democratic traditions. A clearer look into the complex web of imperialist expansion revealed that the same technologies and mechanisms of statecraft utilized to seize land, dispossess people, and subvert knowledge production in the name of resource extraction were strikingly similar in Black communal spaces throughout the world.

What also became readily apparent was that these practices were continually rehearsed and refined within Black communities and then exported to other non-Black, nonwestern regions. The relational dynamics of western imperial projects that focused on the environment as a whole and carcerality (by way of militarism) were revealed through the radical orientation of organizing strategies which demanded absolute change to the violent structured hierarchies inherent within the western civil project. Resultantly, the methodologies mobilized through radical organizing made apparent the fragile nature of hierarchical formations present within western epistemological traditions. The heavy-handed nature of western imposition either through means of statecraft or brute militarism had two objectives: destabilization and resource extraction.

Through tireless strategic efforts that included political education and coalition building, organizing efforts led to the development of a coherent network of communal spaces that very clearly understood the logics that bound together resource extraction and militarism. The archives of radical organizing also revealed the need to decenter provincial analyses that highlighted one particular region as the epicenter of strategy and model building. Such an exercise strongly pushed against the reactionary nature of the state apparatus which was coalescing against radicalism in the formation of philanthropic / nongovernmental organization (NGO) partnerships that served to reinforce hierarchical formations through the inscription of pejorative blackness. However, such mechanizations are important in the context of the environmental/carceral relationship as the NGO sector would take root within the imperial centers of material extraction, namely transnational energy corporations seeking to destabilize those mobilizing against the imperial practice of resource extraction.

The partnerships among philanthropic actors, NGOs, and the formal state were situated as interlocutors of mass disruption and counterintelligence propaganda schemes in the lives of Black communities. While such efforts took time to develop in the realm of carcerality as a specific site, the coalescence of the aforementioned triumvirate played a major role in the regions where resource extraction was prominent. In a reactionary manner, the state attempted to silence the demands for political, economic, and social autonomy from the parasitic dynamics of western extraction. At the heart of these demands was a consistent thread that brought to the fore the multiple ways resource extraction countered existing knowledge traditions. These knowledge traditions positioned a vastly different relationship among the land, people, and resources, and demanded an end to practices that were causing harm to communal spaces, resources, and people. While these traditions were varied in nature and did not all follow the same modality of implementation, they were all highly attuned to the effects of the regional dynamics that governed the precarious relationship between the environment (specifically resources) and life.

A primary aim of racial capitalism was to prevent the proliferation of a logic that affirmed any position of autonomy that did not center itself on the right of violent extraction. Given the fraught dynamics between Black communities and racial capitalist endeavors, two strategies were developed as a means to circumvent the legitimacy of Black knowledge production. The first, and most direct, was the propping up of a particular individual or group through means of momentary benevolence in return for unabashed support of imperial projects. Such a strategy often brought the heavy hand of western intellectual traditions in the form of military and/or paramilitary operations that were installed to suppress knowledge production that did not acquiesce to the basest forms of resource extraction. The intimate connection between matters of warfare/terror/violence and extraction of resources was a clear pattern wrought by the mechanizations of western nation-building. To this end, the tactical maneuvering of finance, energy, and land capital was undergirded by and informed the military wing of the nation apparatus.

The second and more circuitous strategy was the attempted ideological manipulation fostered through the inner workings of the NGO, philanthropic, and state collective. The articulation presented by this grouping was a positioning of racial capitalist principles at the heart of a counterintelligence framework. Through the establishment of faux communal spaces, founding of schools, funding of clinics, and the propagandizing of specific labor- and gender-based policy initiatives, there was an explicit attempt afoot to simultaneously center the logics of western traditions and also make illegible Black knowledge traditions.

As replicated throughout the contours of imperialist endeavors, the establishment of these tactics was done through the vehicle of a civil project that was immersed within the establishment of the human as a governing paradigm. At the center of the civil project was the reification of hierarchical schema that made natural the logic of violent extraction. These efforts positioned extraction and the predictable horrific consequences as a two-sided coin—either an unfortunate but desperately valuable process in the advancement of the human condition or an all-encompassing, omniscient monolith that could and should not be displaced—as it was the stabilizing presence within an otherwise uncivilized landscape. The only way to make change or limit reform was through the channels of the civil project which would inevitably reproduce the violent processes of environmental destabilization propagated by western imperialism.

As marked within the annals of radical organizing, the reactionary measures taken by the state via the coalescence of racial capitalism in order to destabilize the environment was a highly instructive moment for understanding the logic of imperialist ambitions. In the rampant buildup of the carceral state, political study of carcerality expanded beyond the provincial civil narratives of crime and punishment as a matter of individualized moral failure. There was a push to understand the connective tissue that bound the many-headed hydra of racial capitalist endeavors. Utilizing the environmental resource model as a blueprint, radical organizing pieced together the relationship among policing/militarization and resource extraction/environmental destabilization, and NGO/philanthropy/civil infrastructure and counterprogramming.

The resultant strategies that were developed as a result of such analysis situated a dynamic where the nodes of racial capitalism were critical sites in understanding the full scope and intentions of carceral development. The connections among seemingly disparate pairings such as the rural/urban, coastal/inland, labor / labor displaced were critical in understanding the totality of the carceral regime. Further, the displacement logics that were associated with resource extraction were highly instructive in understanding the state's reliance upon militarization via policing and a highly fraught carceral system of prisons, jails, criminal courts, prosecutors, and probation/parole officers. Within such an expansive view, the material logics of violent oil extraction/continuation within Black communities were part and parcel of the warfare tactics deployed by the agents of racial capitalism.

5

Policing Health and Safety

From the middle of the 1980s and running through the 1990s, the Los Angeles Police Department operated a highly controversial program know as "Undercover Buy." Touted as a drug diversion resource, the program placed LAPD officers on the high school campuses across Los Angeles County with the explicit purpose of convincing high school students to purchase drugs—most commonly marijuana—from the officers. Once the transaction was completed, the students would be detained, taken to the appropriate official on the school grounds, very often an assistant principal or counselor, and subsequently expelled from school. The expulsion from school was at the behest of the LAPD, who made an agreement with the school district that the students would not be arrested, the expulsion from school functioning as a satisfactory form of discipline. While high school principals and board representatives green-lit the program, many did not know, or claimed they did not know, the inner workings of the program. One of the details was that a majority of those expelled were done for making small-scale purchases, often for less than five dollars' worth of drugs, from undercover officers.

Investigations by organizations such as Coalition Against Police Abuse and Urban Research Policy Institute revealed that the students very often rebuffed offers to purchase drugs by the officers, but were continually pressured, nevertheless.* It was also revealed that many of the students were Black and were purposely sought out because of their lack of willingness to push back against the undercover officers' overtures. It was also their first time purchasing and/or taking drugs. The CAPA report also went on to document how several organizations that had been working with Black health care workers to develop holistic treatment programs to assist youth struggling with various addictions faced severe obstacles introduced by the LAPD. For example, unless organizations were in lockstep with or advocated for the LAPD's drug-as-crime model, it was very difficult to establish meaningful partnerships with schools in order to provide support for youth. Counter to framing addiction and general drug use as a criminal justice issue that demanded the intervention of police, judges, and prisons, this coalition of community organizations and health care workers situated drug use and addiction as a public health concern (in the case of severe addiction) and/or a recreational leisure activity akin to alcohol use.

Ironically, it was under the guise of protecting the health of youth that Undercover Buy was initiated. School board member Roberta Weintraub, a staunch antibusing advocate, hailed the

---

* The Urban Policy Research Institute was an organization helmed by Dr. Mae Churchill. Dedicated to the ending of carcerality as a modality of governance, UPRI was at the forefront of documenting, organizing, and planning against the various mechanizations of carceral state terror. UPRI worked together with a range of collectives throughout Southern California and conducted extensive community-based projects that sought to undo the logics of the carceral state. Working at the early epochal formation of carceral governance, UPRI was a steadfast opponent to the several attempts by a burgeoning carceral enterprise to enclose the freedom and movement of Black people within Southern California.

success of Undercover Buy and strongly rebuked a call to halt the program. Defending the program, Weintraub stated, "At a time when the state of California on a bipartisan basis is moving forward to make sure our children are safe from drug addiction, we're moving backwards." The tension between community organizers, parents, and teachers on one side and members of the school board, police, and elected officials on the other revealed the convergence between health and the carceral state. Black community organizations throughout the 1980s and 1990s pressed against the logics of a rapid encroachment of state surveillance and entrapment programs under the guise of health and safety. Undercover Buy was representative of such a confluence and indicative of a group of systems that were directly implicated in the degradation of Black health.

Health and Blackness

The specter of premature death is constant within the paradigmatic dynamics of western epistemological projects levied against Black life. During the carceral epoch, the challenges have been plenty: coping with grief, mobilizing to secure material resources, and navigating moments of uncontrollable suffering are but a few. In contradistinction to the logics of racial capitalism, rather than focus on the intentionality of death, Black radical organizers framed their theories and organizing strategies on the development and maintenance of life-affirming pathways and traditions. Given the countervailing approach of the framework, there was a demand to understand the nuances associated with death-inducing technologies of the state as well as to map out the life-affirming traditions that kept Black communal spaces intact. The traditions of Black knowledge production had roots that extended deeper than western thought and thus were much more robust. A blended methodological pursuit, the tactics were informed by decolonial practices and thus spanned time, geography, and western constructions of being. Concomitantly, the evidence collected by radical organizing revealed that the perverse rationale of the carceral regime was much more sinister than containment and removal. Like prior modalities of racial capitalist governance, the focus of western traditions under the blueprint of the human archetype was corporal and thus the inscription of pejorative blackness into the social arrangement followed suit.

The framing of carcerality as the logical extension of the ideological and material military apparatus was a constant thread within the inner workings of Black radical archives. Specifically, there was a consistent question that arose within meetings, workshops, and correspondence among organizers and community members: *What are the life-affirming possibilities when confronting a structural apparatus that is designed to destroy the constitutive elements of life itself?* Rather than an inquiry of existential dimensions, the question provided a framework that informed the basis of organizing. As a result, there was an insistent focus on understanding the effect that multiscalar structural violence/terror had upon the overall well-being of Black communities. Such an analysis rendered that policing/militarization was not merely about the harm emanating from physical violence, but also about the systems of health and types of health treatment available to Black communities.

A main inquiry that was posed in trying to understand the relationship between health and the buildup of a vast carceral infrastructure was the following: *What do health and well-being mean in the midst of extreme terror levied against Black communities?* Examination of the intimate relationship between Black health and carcerality focused on the utilization of, experimentation on, and destruction of Black subjects in the clutches of the carceral project. Tracing this epistemological lineage, the carceral archives reveal that the intent of these violent methodological pursuits was to craft the perfect human subject through dehumanization. This was not an anomaly; virtually all forms of carcerality sought to dissociate Black people from their bodies in profound capacities. Pushing the outer limits of western epistemological imagination, the sheer madness unleashed upon Black people during the buildup of the carceral epoch in the name of health and science became central to western imperial projects.

Health and Archival Violence

Organizing collectives were able to map the scope of these experimentative, terroristic projects and connect the proverbial dots across imagined national boundaries. Given the decolonial framework applied by radical organizing, a path formed that linked the carceral/militaristic project to a grotesque fascination with black bodies. As an organizing strategy, the dissemination of these bodily centered projects was situated alongside the development of health care administration. Within this paradigm, the physical clutches of the carceral state functioned as a laboratory in consistent dialogue with governing state structures. The solidification of this relationship resulted in key state structures being granted the civil power to adjudicate over the bodily concerns of black subjects. Including education, social services, housing, and justice, virtually all large state structures had adjudication capacity over Black subjects. While the civil project framed these projects as matters of health and health care, the underlying philosophy that governed these structural capacities was violence-based disciplinary (re)actions against Black communities and their adherent knowledge traditions. The sordid details of the carceral archive, including the testing of experimental medication, psychological behavioral protocols, and effects of highly addictive mind-altering drugs, indicate the extent to which violence inflicted upon black bodies was done with the explicit purpose of scientific manipulation in the creation of a permanent racial hierarchy.

The effect of the relationship of the disciplinary aspects between carcerality and health resulted in two distinct frameworks with respect to the civil apparatus. The first framework solidified a paradigm of pejorative blackness that rendered blackness as a constant state of nonhuman subjectivity. The vast projects that emanated from the dynamics of the medical/health/scientific infrastructure resulted in civil processes that defined blackness as always in a position of negative relationality to the human. Within the hierarchal structure of the civil, blackness was both relational and within the scope of western rationality, objectively the abject baseline. Situated within a Sisyphean paradox, blackness could not outmaneuver a tightly constructed ideological conundrum that permanently tied it to the logic of death as predetermined/ normal. In gross irony, the violence that was meted out against blackness via the carceral/science project was inscribed into the civic mindscape/blueprint as a permanent status. The individual ethos of the civic project further obscured the inner workings of the state and placed the locus of violence onto Black communities. Thus, pejorative blackness became the reason for all the ill-fated medical and health calamities within Black communities. Further, the framings of indicators of health in western modalities of life were positioned on a scale relation to blackness. As in prior epochs, pejorative blackness became that which was not healthy or best suited for a high quality of life.

The response by Black communities to this confluence was distrust and instructive distancing from the tentacles of the state. The Black communal response to the death-inducing capacity of the state was the immersion into traditions of healing, collective organizing, and evading the proverbial radar of state power.

While much of western knowledge production has attempted to erase the logics of Black knowledge production from the civic imagination, they remained at the core of Black strategies for the creation of life. The central aspect to the maintenance of these traditions was the development of autonomous structures that provided the conditions for Black people to thrive. Utilizing long-held spiritual and cultural practices, Black communities relied upon an internal system that informed the vast possibilities for sustaining life. Developed as communal institutions, these formations became critical to the dissemination of information and practices that allowed for Black communities to live. Building upon the border-crossing logics of Black communal existence, Black communities engaged in a shared knowledge space that informed the growth and development of spiritual and cultural practices affirming Black life, connecting the built environment to both the spiritual and the corporal and stressing the importance of interconnectivity to the sustaining of life.

Autonomous Black life-affirming traditions greatly informed the organizing strategies that were central to Black sustenance during the advent of the carceral era. The basis of the collective organizing platform was informed by three key principles: the connection between the mind and body, the political education of health, and the framing of life as supreme to capital accumulation. Political education was vital to the development of a robust organizing strategy against the logics of the carceral era. The tactics of such educative practices branched into two distinct formations. The first was marking and disseminating the malicious intentions of racial capitalism with respect to matters of medical/scientific methodological violence. The second was the implementation of strategies on behalf of Black communal organizations and members seeking immediate redress from the state governance structures. One of the primary ways this was done was through organizing community members with representation to file claims and win material judgments against the state.

Health and Organizing against the Carceral State

The western epistemological project to render Black knowledge traditions illegible was most pronounced in attempts to silence Black experiential knowledges of the medical/scientific infrastructure. Often configured within the realm of conspiracy, there was a multitiered platform that reified western modalities of truth and simultaneously espoused claims that reified pejorative blackness. Radical Black organizing collectives, understanding the nuances of this dynamic, undertook the responsibility to give life to these experiences. Through a rigorous process of collecting, sharing, and disseminating these narratives, the Black experience became the centerpiece of knowledge production. Further, through clandestine network building, organizers were able to obtain damning reports, dossiers, and state testimony that detailed the violence of the medical industry. Such information was critical in the development of a pedagogy that informed workshop development, protest rallies, and debunking the mythical claims of state benevolence. As a matter of coalition building, the information proved vital in mapping out the scope of western modalities of violence across geographic settings.

The second intervention involved restitution and recompense for the effects of state violence. These practices were strategically chosen to provide material support for Black communities impacted by violence emanating from the carceral/medical enterprise. Utilizing a cadre of trusted legal professionals and policy advocates, the organizers focused on documenting the state's complicity in the destruction of Black life. Realizing that such strategies were not going to develop long-term radical change, the goals of such tactics were to attain the largest and most sweeping form of material resource allocation from the state to Black communities. Secondarily, to counter the propaganda apparatus of the state, there was an intention to mark state violence within the channels of state dissemination. Never counted as a "victory," the basis of these claims formed a counternarrative that would further expose the gaping holes in the state's mythmaking apparatus.

Given that various state structures had the ability to enact discipline via the capillaries of the medical/health infrastructure, organizational and communal strategies involved removal from the tracking mechanisms/mandates/adjudications that were central to the buildup of the carceral state. Organizational, communal logics validated the imperative to not participate within the structural apparatuses which demanded violence upon Black people. From mandatory prescriptions to forced sterilizations as a precondition for access to material resources, to the separation of families on the basis of psychological profiles, Black communities framed these practices as violent, illogical, and counterintuitive to the life-affirming traditions that informed Black knowledge production. Rather than abiding by a violence-inducing structure, Black communities strategically absconded from the state to avoid the violence that flowed from it.

The struggle to maintain a hold on life-affirming traditions during the rampant structural violence predicated on premature death was a constant tension for Black radical organizing and community projects. However, such tension revealed the larger and much more insidious pursuits of carcerality as a dominant model of governance while illustrating the profound capacity of Black knowledge traditions to sustain community in the midst of violent warfare.

6

Liberation

This chapter is based on material from the Clyde Adrian Woods and Mothers Reclaiming Our Children collections. Clyde Woods was a geographer and Black Studies scholar whose work centered on the foregrounding of the Black working class's material and cultural traditions. The majority of Woods's published research was centered in the US South, with a particular focus on the Mississippi Delta. He famously developed the conceptualization of Blues Epistemology as a means of documenting the social vision of Black liberation from the clutches of what he described as the "plantation bloc." Prior to his passing in 2011, Woods was working on a manuscript detailing Black communal organizing and life in Los Angeles. Like his work in the Mississippi Delta, Woods's research pulled from a variety of sources including musicians, community scholars, visual artists, policymakers, private developers, and the hidden hands of the state. The Woods collection at the Southern California Library contains the very essence of ontological practices that give life to Black intellectual thought and study.

The Mothers Reclaiming Our Children collection emanates from a collective of mothers whose children were ensnared within the confines of the carceral state. Forged during the 1990s to confront the state, Mothers ROC sought to undo the inherent logics of the carceral state. With a framework that centered the displacement and dispossession of Black life as critical to understanding the development and expansion of the carceral state, Mothers ROC established coalition building across a broad base of support throughout disparate geographic regions of the state. Informed by a politics that sought to fundamentally undo the carceral state and redistribute state resources in a radically democratic manner, Mothers ROC was critical to the articulation and study of the carceral state as an apparatus that tethered seemingly incongruent regions together across space and time.

Conspiracy and Carceral State Schemes

Pieced together from newspaper accounts, internal memos, and raw video, an account emerges of one of the more surreal events to unfold in the heart of Black Los Angeles. In November 1996, an unusual meeting was held on the campus of Alain Locke High School, located in the Watts section of Los Angeles, California. The director of the Central Intelligence Agency (CIA), John Deutch, addressed an over-capacity auditorium about the CIA's role in the distribution of crack cocaine in South Central Los Angeles. The mass of Black attendees listened as Deutch attempted to explain away the narrative that had unfolded weeks before as a result of the bombshell report from Gary Webb of the *San Jose Mercury News*. Webb's story revealed to the nation what had been common knowledge for Black people in South Central Los Angeles for the better part of a decade. The United States government was directly implicated in the smuggling of cocaine and weapons into the region. When relayed from the mouths of Black Angelinos, the connection was dismissed as a crazy conspiracy theory. How and why would the US government facilitate the transfer of drugs into its own cities? Following the cultural moral ethos established during the Reagan-Bush-Clinton presidential administrations of the 1980s and early '90s, the drug culture was framed as a "cop-out" for Black people not wanting to take responsibility for their alleged lack of a work ethic and proclivity toward violence and crime. Webb shook the ideological fault line and exposed one of the biggest acts of targeted state terror of the late twentieth century. Given the events that unfolded during the 1992 Los Angeles Rebellion, the United States government was in full panic mode over the fear that Black people would once again take to the streets and revolt. In typical reactionary posturing and under the guise of damage control, Deutch was sent to Watts in an attempt to assuage the community's anger. The exact opposite occurred. The crowd shouted down Deutch's pedestrian attempts to stymie concerns and distance the CIA from Webb's reporting.

Tensions ran particularly high when a middle-aged white man took to the microphone. He followed a long line of Black people who narrated experience after experience of having nefarious interactions with the police. Stories ranged from drugs planted in vehicles to having witnessed the mysterious appearance of a large cache of weapons and ammunition left in empty train cars along railroad tracks running through the heart of South Central Los Angeles. In a rather monotonous and straight-ahead cadence, the man identified himself as Michael Ruppert, a former officer of the Los Angeles Police Department (LAPD). He then gave a first-hand account of having direct knowledge of the LAPD's scheme to funnel drugs into the city and stated that he worked with key individuals who would disperse drugs to conspirers who would then spread them throughout the city in return for a reduced sentence or immunity. Ruppert's testimony was followed by an eruption of applause and loud shouting from the crowd as the moderator attempted to quiet the auditorium.

While the response could be misinterpreted as validation of
the testimony of a former agent of the state coming to the defense of an aggrieved community, the material from the radical
collective reveals that such an interpretation would be a severe
misreading of the communal dynamics. Rather, the crowd was
affirming what was already culturally understood the moment
the gathering was announced. The parading of the FBI in front of
Black residents was merely a spectacle, an attempt to save face in a
moment of desperation in light of the events that further exposed
the illegitimacy of the carceral state. The response from the crowd
was an affirmation of the circus that had been paraded as a hearing
that day in Watts. Ruppert's testimony was evidence of how far
afield the state had gone: that a former agent of one of the most
repressive regional regimes (Southern California) had decided
to relinquish the material benefits of the carceral state in favor
of the ontological practices espoused by Black radical thought.

Very simply, Ruppert's and Webb's accounts were built upon
decades-long narratives, testimonials, legal proceedings, and
physical confrontations by Black people over and against various agents of the carceral apparatus. The Woods and Mothers
ROC collections reveal through handwritten notes, newspaper
stories, lawsuits, and a myriad of sourced material the nefarious plans of the state apparatus to cause material harm to Black
communities. In addition to the infamous stories of powdered
cocaine being left in the middle of the Nickerson Gardens and
Imperial Courts housing projects in Watts, there were countless
stories of police planting large quantities of cocaine in alleyways,
bus stops, and cars.

The logic that undergirded such reality for Black residents
was labeled as conspiratorial at best. Although it was common
sense within the organizing logic of Black communal formations,
the agents of the state deemed it a threat and thus attempted to
marginalize its legitimacy. Thus, on that day in 1996, the eruption
from the crowd was a collective knowing of the state coming apart

at the seams. Similarly, the fates of Ruppert and Webb reflected the reactionary response to the knowledge traditions of drug and weapon importation within Black communities throughout Los Angeles: at best their reports and testimony were characterized as conspiratorial as mainstream news outlets assisted in the CIA's attempts to erase them.

Strategy Development and Warcraft

As evidenced in archival documents in the Southern California Library, a scheme of facilitating and profiting from drug sales was undertaken to fund a US–backed war against the Sandinista government in Nicaragua who held close ties with other socialist countries in Central America and the Caribbean as well as the USSR. Agents of the US defense apparatus, including the CIA, entered into a triangular trade whereby they facilitated the movement of drugs from Central America into Los Angeles, used the money garnered through the drug trade to purchase weapons from Iran, and then used those weapons to bolster a highly manufactured opposition, the Contras, who sought to destabilize the Sandinistas through violent warfare.

The gross irony during this illicit trade was that the concurrent federally funded "War on Drugs" was targeting the city of Los Angeles. The LAPD, who assisted in the facilitation of drugs, was simultaneously given federal and state funds to arrest and lock up Black people who were distributing the very same drugs. Webb's account brought to the fore knowledge Black people were long familiar with, and while such reporting slightly removed the veil for a larger audience, it also revealed the true intent of the state apparatus: the suppression and containment of the Black community.

This multifaceted process also revealed the much more sinister reality that the state in this capacity could not be reformed. Whole units within the government were implicated, and the logics of the civil apparatus did not present a process by which the government would indict, prosecute, convict, and remove itself from authority. Thus, the levers of government, as evident by CIA Director Deutch's comments before the packed crowd at Alain Locke High School, attempted to erase and create an alternative truth that would further diminish Black knowledge traditions.

Black intellectual and knowledge traditions in Los Angeles immediately and consistently identified the perpetuator of terror within their communities as the state—and thus were deemed irrational by the violent logics of western imperial endeavors. Black intellectual traditions were (and continue to be) crucial in assessing the root logics of western philosophical traditions that are predicated upon and make normative the violent exploitative tendencies of western imperialism. In the case of the CIA's funneling of drugs into Southern California, a key aspect in the archives of Black communal organizing was the connections that were forged via Black communities in Los Angeles and Nicaragua. These connections revealed a systematic effort across geographic borders to displace Black people from the land, extract resources, and suppress Black knowledge traditions, all facilitated by processes of state governance at the behest of racial capitalist interests. Meeting throughout North and Central America, Black collectives conducted community information sessions, studied together, and tirelessly pieced together the inner workings of a war-making western imperial project. One of the primary solutions put forward by organizations in both regions was to demand autonomy from the state in order to create their own parameters of governance and to remove the yoke of dogged state-facilitated terror. It is through such collective action that Black intellectual traditions proved yet again vital to the development of radically democratic, egalitarian social formations that are invested in the processes of liberation.

Liberation

Liberation is a word / campaign term that is constantly used within the archives of radical organizing collectives. Rather than freedom or rights, liberation carries with it a process, an undoing, a building to something. Liberation also conveys that the yoke of oppression can be named and, through such naming, studied as a means to prevent reproduction of said oppression and cooptation of liberatory strategies and efforts. Liberation is also a multidimensional space that entails the structuring of ontologies fundamental to undoing oppressive tactics and regimes.

The brute physical manifestation of state violence has been central to the narrative of the carceral era and carcerality as the dominant modality of governance. As a spectacle, the implementation of gross physical violence has been instrumental in organizing against the draconian nature of carcerality. Specifically, the spectacle of violent action by the state as the facilitator, perpetuator, and manifestation of structural and interpersonal violence in the lives of Black communities is the flashpoint that brings cohesion in efforts to fight against carcerality. Yet, it is the spectacle—the moment of the spectacular—that has also facilitated the continuance of the carceral project as the key modality of state life. The spectacle is that which can easily be incorporated into the mechanizations of the civic as outliers to normative processes of state governance. The consistent response of the state has been to position the spectacular into the heart of a civic process that rests within the pejorative black law-and-order subject-making project and mutes the existence of systemic structures as the primary conduits of racial-making and racial violence. The spectacle is thus absorbed through individual morality claims that situate acts of spectacular violence as the province of those who have betrayed a mythical oath to the human (in common parlance referred to as "bad apples") and provide a façade for state violence. As a result, formations of spectacular violence become incorporated into the boundaries of civic possibility, and thus, the normative framework of what grotesque violence continually expands. As cautioned by organizations such as CAPA, the incorporation of the vile beating of Rodney King at the hands of the LAPD as captured on video by George Holliday had the potential to change the terms of debate so that: (1) video evidence would always be needed to prove claims that Black people have known and experienced to be true and (2) the constant rendering of the spectacle (the violent attack on Rodney King) over and over again across news outlets and media platforms would numb the collective psyche. Thus the spectacle would grow to become begrudgingly (or in some quarters very willingly) accepted as a part of normative society. As a result, while the moment of the spectacle was key for organizing purposes, the spectacle was understood to be emblematic of carceral state governance practices.

In the struggle for liberation, radical collective knowledge formation has pushed for a rigorous analysis of the quotidian manifestations of state governance. A framework focused upon the quotidian reveals that the spectacle is both a product of and a mask concealing the multifaceted nature of carceral terror as a source of energy for racial capitalist projects. On the first account, the spectacle becomes spectacular as cohesion against quotidian forms of state terror crystallizes into a visceral formation. A rejection of the civic, the cohesion exposes the brutal logic of western epistemological traditions and pulls back the veil to expose the fragility of the human project, revealing the absurd normative standards that have absorbed previous spectacles as a core aspect of state governance. As a product of the quotidian, the formation of the spectacular rests within knowledge traditions that are based upon a multiplicity of being. Such an ontology situates the rationale of western state governance traditions as tentacles of terror designed with a specific task of reinforcing binary modalities central to the human.

Yet the spectacle also works to mask the many dimensions that are at the generative core of the carceral regime. Western epistemological traditions operate within the mythical realm of linear pathways based upon invented historical creations. Such creations are marked by specific spectacles that function as a conduit to transition from one moment/achievement/crisis to the next. Within such a framework, the spectacle becomes the proxy for understanding nation-building and, importantly, the development of the human as a natural process. Read within its normative gaze, the spectacle within the realm of carcerality can also function as a turning point for state growth and building after a moment of crisis. It is within these reactionary moments that the state attempts to transform the spectacular into an isolated event solely related to the spectacle, as in the 1965 Watts and 1992 Los Angeles Rebellions. The intense focus on the spectacle attempts to prevent the root cause—the quotidian—of state terror from being articulated as a highly structured apparatus that implements violence through several conduits, with brute force being just one of many.

It is here, at the locus of the spectacular as a coherent formation and of the state in a reactionary posture, that the role of political education is critical to radical organizing knowledge production. Political education is immersed in genealogies that expand beyond the borders/limitations of racial capitalist myths. Central to the ethos of political education is a process of coalition building that is neither comfortable nor shortsighted. There is an intentional positioning of various ways of being together as a collective to comprehend the perverse logics of normative hierarchal implementation and maintenance. Further, the liberatory praxis that undergirds coalition building is informed by an ontological framing of liberation as a constantly ongoing practice. The vision of liberation, which encompasses the experiences, strategies, and complexity of the multitude, is immersed in a genealogy of time that is not predicated upon nation-building exercises of conquest and extraction. A disavowal of history as a linear formation, liberation can only be achieved by a radical undoing of the apparatus that governs both the structural and the ideological imperatives that shape interpersonal dynamics. Thus, political education teaches that modalities of liberation will not come in the shape of easy victories, nor will they be achieved by means of state acquiescence. Rather, liberation will take shape through the rigorous plotting of ontological traditions that carry the burden of existing in many dimensions across many spaces throughout the many understandings of time. The CAPA archive reveals that it was firmly understood that the establishment of the 1992 Gang Truce was predicated upon keeping intact the structural logic and ontological presence of Black communal organizing such as the Crips and Bloods throughout Los Angeles. While city, county, and state officials and representatives positioned the Crips and Bloods as the centerpiece of civic malfeasance, CAPA positioned the Crips and Bloods as part of an ontology of resistance and renewal that was immersed in love of Blackness and Black communities. As documented by CAPA, the organizing strategies of the Crips and Bloods represented a severe threat to racial capitalist seats of power in the region and thus were systematically attacked by virtually every technology at the state's disposal (including infiltration and psychological and physical forms of domestic warfare). CAPA understood that the governing principles of Black communal organizations took on a character completely different from western standards. That which was given primacy—an intense love of neighborhood and family—dictated a completely different way of being that did not cohere with the exploitative logics that were central to racial capitalist ontological practices.

Such a reckoning of western epistemology and its adherents demands a rigorous grappling with those traditions that have been made illegible, erased, or silenced. Political education becomes the key driver to wade through the complexity of knowledge traditions that are at times contradictory and in tension with one another. Within such a framework, political education is the vital component that allows the spectacular to sustain its cohesive nature and not be seduced by the material and ideological lures presented by and through the logics of racial capitalism.

Within the contemporary framework of the carceral regime, the major tenets of racial capitalism have sought to unseat the knowledge traditions that have been central to the production of Black epistemologies. Understanding the tendencies of racial capitalism, radical organizing principles have positioned Blackness as the main conduit toward a liberatory future. Placing Blackness at the center of methodological and strategic pursuits situates Black ontologies and practices at the core of actions, platforms, and engagement with the state and Black communities. The spaces, schools of thought, and ways of being that have been established by Black communities are firmly positioned as the locus of movement-building and liberation efforts. While the logics of the civil project demand a discarding of Black traditions that are rooted within multiple ways of being, radical organizing philosophy demands an open embrace of Black traditions as the only possible road toward a liberatory future. The positionality of Black radical subjectivity is strategic in that it squarely situates the cooptative tendencies of a racial capitalist enterprise that demands the collaboration of racialized junior partners as an impediment to liberation.

Understanding the scope and intent of the ideological and material trappings of imperialist endeavors, the logic of Black knowledge productions situates such racial capitalist impositions as farcical to liberatory practice. The centering of Blackness entails a structuring of the mind that cannot conceive of the violent exploitative tendencies of western epistemological traditions as viable life-affirming practices. Very simply, the overtures made by the state via racialized cooptation do not register on the spectrum of possibility and are cast as delusional. The location of Blackness at the core thus demands a restructuring of the mind in a manner that opens up myriad possibilities.

Conclusion

Series 1

A sample from a group of documents from the Coalition Against Police Abuse (CAPA) and the Urban Policy Research Institute (UPRI) describes tension related to the discovery of a secret, hypersurveillant focused division within the Los Angeles Police Department—the Public Disorder Intelligence Division (PDID). PDID was found to have been in existence for roughly fifty years (between the 1920s through the end of the 1970s) and worked to infiltrate, cause friction within, and surveil organizations that were deemed to be a threat to proper civil engagement. Through countless lawsuits, multi-coalition organizing efforts, and unfettered determination, the sheer scope and function of PDID was revealed to the public.

APRIL 25, 1975

STATEMENT OF THE CITIZENS' COMMITTEE OF
INQUIRY INTO LOS ANGELES LAW ENFORCEMENT
INTELLIGENCE PRACTICES CONCERNING THE
PROPOSED STANDARDS AND PROCEDURES FOR
THE PUBLIC DISORDER INTELLIGENCE DIVISION
OF THE LOS ANGELES POLICE DEPARTMENT

The Citizens' Committee on L.A. Law Enforcement Intelligence
Practices has reviewed the proposed guidelines in the context
of the forty year history of politicalintelligence gathering
by the L.A.P.D., and in the light of the recent nation-wide
disclosures of official misuse ob both intelligence data and
intelligence operatives. In our review we have tried to judge
how well the guidelines protect citizens from intrusions into
their personal lives, their political thoughts, activities and
associations. Before these guidelines are considered for
acceptance we feel that the numerous deficiencies of the document
must be publicly examined by this body and by the citizens
of Los Angeles.

Contrary to the the stated view of the Mayor, the Police Commissioners and others in the city, we found the guidelines not
to be an advance over past procedures. We found the the definitions supplied to be nebulous and open to the widest and
most abusive interpretations; we-found that, in fact, political
"Thought" was still be used as a basis for inclusion in such
files, and we found that there were significant ommissions
from the guidelines. The following statement raises questions
about the areas we feel are most important for investigation and
discussion:

ON BASIC DEFINITIONS

1. Who is to define what acts are ideologically motivated?
2. Who is to define what acts may result in a disruption of the
   public order?
3. Are gatherings of more than one person in front of a building
   which may result in the blocking of a citizen's access to
   that place an act of public disorder? Is a picket line?
4. Is mere participation in a demonstration which ended up being
   declared an "illegal gathering" enough of a basis for inclusion?
5. Is advocating or planning such a demonstration sufficient for
   an organization or individual to be included?
6. And if the police, themselves, were the ones to declare an act
   or demonstration an illegal gathering, can they be expected to
   be the sole definers of what is, for the purpose of the files,
   to be considered advocacy or participation in an act of public
   disruption?
7. Is this not a merging of the legislative and administrative function?

ON THE PURPOSE OF THE PDID
We question the very existence of a division whose purpose is to

Figure 1. "Statement of the Citizens' Committee of Inquiry into
Los Angeles Law Enforcement Intelligence Practices concerning
the Proposed Standards and Procedures for the Public Disorder
Intelligence Division of the Los Angeles Police Department." 1975.
Courtesy of the Southern California Library.

● THE

RAP
SHEET Nov. - Dec. 1979

● Published By The
Citizen's Commission on Police Repression
633 S. Shatto Pl. Suite 200, Los Angeles 90005   387-3937

● Motion For New Trial in Pratt Case

To observers of FBI counter intelligence (COINTELPRO) activities, tne case of Elmer (Geronimo) Pratt is the most significant and outrageous since the killings of Black Panthers Fred Hampton and Mark Clark in Chicago. The trutn in the Pratt case has taken years--through twisted roads and suppressed evidence--to come to light. What began as a frame-up for murder, on slight evidence, is now a singular example of the extremes to which the FBI will go to destroy a political activist and disrupt a political movement.

In 1972, Black Pantner Geronimo Pratt was convicted of murder in a celebrate trial dubbed the "Santa Monica tennis court murder." Four years earlier, in December 1968, two black men held up a young couple, Caroline and Kenneth Olsen, playing tennis. They took $30, and then shot them both. The wife died, but the husband lived, later to be a witness against Pratt.

The original eye-witness accounts by the husband of two clean-shaven men, did not fit Pratt, who had a moustache and goatee. Furthermore--as was later testified to at the trial--Pratt had not been in Los Angeles at the time of the murder. In
(Cont'd. p.2)

Suit Wins Files -- Plaintiffs Gagged

Fifteen months and three judges after the filing of C.A.P.A. et.al. v Gates, the ACLU-sponsored lawsuit against LAPD infiltration of lawful political groups has produced its first significant court order--a discovery order. On Nov. 7, 1979, Superior Court Judge Harry L. Hupp ordered the LAPD to produce 1200 pages of political intelligence files maintained on the plaintiffs: 7 organizations and 5 individuals. However, the interlocutory (amendable) order imposed an outrageously restrictive "gag order" on what plaintiffs could do with or say about the documents.

The discovery of 1200 pages of LAPD political intelligence documents would be the most significant release ever. But the gag order would restrict the plaintiffs and their attorney to one copy of each document, and plaintiffs would be prohibited from either taking notes from or duplicating that one copy. The court order also prohibits plaintiffs from using the documents in "the promotion of their political or social goals." Anyone who violated the order could be jailed for contempt of court.
(Cont'd. p.3)

★★★★★★★★★★★★★ November Meeting

The Citizen's Commission steering committee will meet on Thursday, November 29th, 7:30 PM in our new office at 633 S. Shatto Pl., upstairs in room 200.

Our educational will feature Sam Kushner, long-time labor activist, writer (Long Road To Delano) and KPFK labor commentator. The topic will be the use of spies and surveillance to neutralize union organizers.

Other agenda items: report on the coordinator's trip to Washington, D.C. (with an update on the FBI Charter) and nominations for a new co-chairperson to replace Jeff Cohen, who has joined our staff. For more information, call Linda or Jeff at 387-3937.

PLEASE NOTE: Due to the holidays, there will be no December Rap Sheet or steering committee meeting. We will re-convene on Thursday, Jan.31st.

We've Moved U⏹

The Citizen's Commission has moved to a larger office on the second floor of the ACLU building at 633 South Shatto Place, Los Angeles. We are now located in Suite 200, and have a new, direct telephone line. Call us at 387-3937, Monday through Friday.

Figure 2. Rap Sheet newsletter published by the Citizens' Commission on Police Repression, Los Angeles. 1979. Courtesy of the Southern California Library.

LOS ANGELES CENTER FOR LAW & JUSTICE

2421 EAST OLYMPIC BOULEVARD
LOS ANGELES, CALIFORNIA 90023
TELEPHONE (213) 266-8690

IN REPLY
PLEASE REFER TO

May 11, 1979

Mr. Stephen Reinhardt, President
Board of Police Commissioners
150-B. Parker Center
150 N. Los Angeles
Los Angeles, CA 90012

RE: COMPLAINT ABOUT PUBLIC DISORDER
INTELLIGENCE DIVISION ACTIVITIES
AT HEARING INTO EULA LOVE SHOOTING
April 25, 1979.

Dear Mr. Reinhardt:

I wish to lodge a formal complaint about the unwarranted intelligence
gathering and surveilance by the LAPD Public Disorder Intelligence
Division (PDID) at the Police Commission hearing on April 25, 1979
regarding the Eula Love shooting.

I personally attended the public hearing held in Room 350 of the
City Hall. While present, I observed two police officers known by
me to be assigned to PDID, Jennifer Drake, Serial No. 14964 and
Carol Hill, Serial No. 14068. Ms. Hill was looking around the room
and then writing something down. I can only surmise she was noting
the presence of those persons who had come to the hearing to observe
and/or voice their opinion on the Eula Love investigation.

I feel that this type of intelligence gathering at a public hearing
is completely inappropriate. The purpose of the hearing, as I understand it, was to give the public an opportunity to present views and
suggestions on LAPD shooting policy to the members of the Police
Commission. However, it defeats this expressed purpose if the police
are gathering intelligence on those who dare to speak out. Further-
more, if the members of the Police Commission allow this type of
activity to go unchecked it casts doubt on your expressed desire to
hear from the community.

I would like to be informed (1) if the intelligence operation was
approved and/or known in advance to members of the Police Commission

Figure 3. "Complaint about Public Disorder Intelligence Division
Activities at Hearing into Eula Love Shooting." Complaint
sent to Stephen Reinhardt, President of the Board of Police
Commissioners. 1979. Courtesy of the Southern California
Library.

Series 2

The CAPA collection houses documentation of early surveillant schema and systems developed in the mid-1970s that were forged through a symbiotic alliance among the LAPD, the United States government (via academic and formal policing institutions), and the aerospace industry. The purpose of this alliance was to craft technological systems that would provide the LAPD with the ability to opaquely monitor and surveil citizens behind the cloak of technology. It is of note that the development of these technological systems occurred as organizations were demanding complete transparency from the LAPD in the wake of the PDID affair.

Figure 4. "Automatic Vehicle Monitoring Systems Study." Report prepared by Jet Propulsion Laboratory, California Institute of Technology, Pasadena, for the National Science Foundation. 1976. Courtesy of the Southern California Library.

INTEROFFICE MEMO   UNCLASSIFIED

LITERATURE SEARCH NO. 74-017   COPY NO. | DATE 10-10-74

TO _____ Bob Sohn _____ SEC. ___393_____

FROM ____ Edmond J. Momjian _____ EXT. __6911____ SEC. ___652_____

SUBJECT ___Advanced Command and Control Systems for Law Enforcement__

    The literature was searched for references concerning command
and control systems for law enforcement and related topics. The
references have been arranged alphabetically by author and have been
divided into the following sections:*

                                                      Page

     I.   Command and Control   1

    II.   Dispatching   8

  III.   Vehicle Location and Identification 15

   IV.   Mobile Digital Communications 24

    V.   Allocation and Deployment 31

   VI.   Police Communications 35

  VII.   General 39

    The following sources of information were covered:

Abstracts and Indexes

    Abstracts on Police Science - March 1974 through August 1974

    Applied Science & Technology Index -
                                      January 1970 through August 1974

    Computer Abstracts - January 1971 through August 1974

    Computing Reviews - January 1973 through August 1974

    Document Retrieval Index - January 1974

    Engineering Index - January 1973 through August 1974

    Government Reports Index - January 1973 through September 1974

    Index to Current Urban Documents -
                              January 1972 through July 1974

Figure 5. "Advanced Command and Control Systems for Law
Enforcement." Jet Propulsion Laboratory (JPL) interoffice memo.
1974. Courtesy of the Southern California Library.

Series 3

Sample documents from the early 1970s taken from the Los Angeles chapter of the Black Panther Party collection reveal the decolonial organizing tendencies of the Panthers. Connecting the colonial struggles in Vietnam to the struggles for Black autonomy in the United States (via food assistance, health care, and job programs), the Panthers demonstrated that just as the US military engages in forms of warfare to attack those who oppose brutal exploitation around the globe, the US state engages in domestic warfare against those it calls "gangs" or "black racists" in the same manner.

You can't keep talking about "peace in Vietnam" and forget about the fight for liberation of black people here at home. Black and brown people are fighting the same army, the same guns, and the same racist attacks as the Vietnamese people. As groups like the Black Panther Party work to meet the needs of the black community, needs which the power structure has been unable and unwilling to meet, they are faced with massive repression.

One day after the Panther Party began their "Breakfast for Children" program in the Westside community, 19 Chicago Panthers, including Bobby Rush, Assistant Minister of Defense, were busted. Charges range from "illegal possession of weapons" to having license plates held on by a piece of wire instead of the "legal" nut and bolt. Fred Hampton, Chairman of the Illinois Panthers, faces 10 charges while Minister Rush faces at least four. This week 21 Panthers were busted in New York City with bail amounting to over 2 million dollars.

The absurdity of the charges and the mass jailings of Panthers shows up the whole thing for exactly what it is--a concentrated effort by the racist power structure to destroy the Black Panther Party nation-ally as well as in Chicago. The reason for this is clear--the powers that be think the Panthers are a threat to their system. The pigs want us to think that the Panthers are a threat to the people--a "gang" of black "racists in reverse". The people of Chicago know this for a lie. We know that the Panthers are fighting for "tho attainment of the needs of the working people and the time when we'll destroy this capitalistic power structure" and begin building a country and a government that serves the needs of all the people.

If we really want to end the war in Vietnam and all other wars in-cluding the one here at home, we must support the struggles of the Black Panthers and other revolutionary groups such as the Young Lords and SDS. One way we can help is to give money--to get the Panthers out of the Chicago prisons, to make it possible for them to continue working. Send money to: Panther Defense Fund, 2350 W. Madison, Chicago, Ill.

Another way to show our support is to attend the trial of Panther Minister Bobby Rush, on Tuesday, April 8. Minister Rush is being tried for gun possession charges. We should be there to show our solidarity, at the Municipal District Court, Midlothian, Ill.

Let's show the cops that we are not going to allow the Panther Party to be liquidated! The people have power when we are together. Let's get together with the Panthers, get them out of jail, and show the courts that their trials will not go unnoticed.

POWER TO THE PEOPLE

                    BLACK POWER TO BLACK PEOPLE
                        LATIN POWER TO LATIN PEOPLE

Figure 6. Message from the Chicago Black Panther Party connecting the war in Vietnam to the war against the Black Panther Party. No date. Courtesy of the Southern California Library.

THE BLACK PANTHER, SATURDAY, APRIL 22, 1972   PAGE 5

20,000 BLACKS VOTE TO CONTROL HOSPITAL
WINSTON-SALEM BLACK COMMUNITY UNITES TO KEEP HOSPITAL FACILITY

Health care for the majority of Black people in Winston-Salem, North Carolina has been in jeopardy for quite some time now. Of the three hospitals in Winston-Salem, one private and two county, Reynolds Memorial, one of the county facilities, is located in East Winston-Salem, the Black community. Reynolds Memorial is one of North Carolina's more modern hospitals, having been built only four years ago at a cost of 7.5 million dollars. Because most Black people are poor and cannot pay for medical attention, Reynolds Memorial has always run on a budget deficit.

This economic condition, unfavorable, of course, to city, county and state administrators, is being rectified through a Health Planning Council, appointed by the county to "plan a health program that would be most beneficial to all residents of Forsyth County" (in which Winston-Salem is located). Since the appointment of the Council, a move has been under-way to phase out Reynolds Memorial Hospital, leaving only a part-time clinic in its place.

The phasing-out has already begun. There is no longer a full-time anesthesiologist, pathologist or surgeon on the Hospital staff, and the full-time technicians have been either fired or have resigned because of the uncertain situation existing at the

After months and months, on April 15th, 20,000 Black people in Winston-Salem, North Carolina, united to get proper medical care.

Hospital. Equipment has been transferred from Reynolds Memorial to the county facility in the Winston-Salem white community, Forsyth Hospital. Also, innovations have been made on the Reynolds Memorial Hospital building to change it to a clinic.

To save what little decent medical care the Winston-Salem Black community was receiving and to protest the racism of the Forsyth County, the United Black Front, made up of various Black community organizations, was formed. Organizations that make up the United Black Front include: The Winston-Salem Branch of the Black Panther Party; Concerned Citizens for Reynolds Memorial Hospital; Comprehensive Health Board, Inc.; NAACP; the Baptist Ministers Conference, and Associates; Winston-Salem Chapter of Black Memorial Day; Welfare Rights Organization; Public Housing Tenant Council Number Four; and

Harambee.

Having exhausted all avenues of redress, the Black United Front has called for a community vote to re-open Reynolds Memorial as a full-time general, acute-care hospital. On Saturday, April 15, 1972, a strong, united Black community, 20,000 in all, came out in the interest of the people.

Like Black and poor communities across this country and around the world, the Winston-Salem Black community's survival is threatened by the capitalists and racists of the U.S. Empire's ruling class. The Black community of Winston-Salem has proven that unity is the key to our survival and to bringing about control of community institutions by the people.

ALL POWER TO THE PEOPLE

BROTHER BARBEE COMMENTS ON SURVIVAL CONFERENCE

April 13, 1972

I attended the Black Community Survival Conference in Oakland and Berkeley, March 29, 30 and 31. It was well-organized, free and successful.

What's more important, the concept of keying a Black Community Conference around basic survival needs like food, clothing and medical care made it possible for a voter registration campaign to become an instant success - over 11,120 registered in three days. I was singely impressed by the community's spontaneous interaction between Black Panther Chairman, Bobby Seale; Sisters Johnnie Tillman, National Chairman, Welfare Rights Organization; Elaine Brown, Black Panther Minister of Information; Ericka Huggins, Black

Wisconsin State Assemblyman LLOYD BARBEE doesn't just talk. He came to California to be at the Black Community Survival Conference.

Panther Party; and Jody Allen, Chairman of the B.S.U., Laney College. The music provided by the Persuasions was more than entertainment to the people who became involved with the words, harmony, rhythm and spirit of this excellent group.

The result was that approximately 17,000 people came together on three different days; received their bags of groceries (with a chicken in every bag); took sickle cell anemia tests and registered to vote at the sites. Community organization and power showed itself for three straight days in the Black Oakland and Berkeley Ghetto.

One clear moral from this conference is that Black Political Power can be marshalled around issues which deeply affect community lives.

Figure 7. "20,000 Blacks Vote to Control Hospital." Black Panther newsletter. 1972. Courtesy of the Southern California Library.

The archival documents in the Southern California Library reveal the multifaceted nature of carcerality as a dominant form of state governance. Beyond the civic apparatus, carcerality is a modality that is intimately connected to the western imperial warfare project. As a result, the state will utilize all structures and nodes of influence to buttress its façade. The reckoning with carcerality as undertaken by radical collectives reveals the state as the bureaucratic driver of a human project invested in violent hierarchies. The result of Black liberatory practice demonstrates that carcerality as an ideological manifestation of state governance is deeply imbricated within all facets of social arrangements. Second and no less important, carcerality is a part of a western rationality that is predicated upon the maintenance of ontological expressions that legitimate bourgeois philosophical adherence to racial capitalism. The development of these expressions is located within the linear narrative of time and progression that fortify the delineation of Blackness from humanity. Read in such a manner, the ideological and material considerations of carcerality as a product of western philosophy situate the structural relationships and inner dynamics of state governance as mechanizations to reproduce the core tenets of the human project for which the suppression of Blackness is of the utmost importance.

As a modality of racial capitalism, one of the key functions of carcerality is to ensure the extractive and exploitative tendencies that undergird western imperialism are held intact. Thus, as read through these series of documents, the logics of the carceral state are designed within an imperialist framework based upon extractive logics such as colonialism and development. The police and military in such a scheme are designed as the brute physical force to ensure ideological adherence and to maintain the exploitative relationship central to the human project. Yet, imperial endeavors such as the carceral state are not omnipotent, and as detailed in the collections of Black radical organizing, points of tension and fragility are ripe for exposure, dismantling, and discarding.

However, what is also evident from the collections is that such work can be achieved only through rigorous study and analysis. Ultimately, the path toward liberation is marked by the need for continued investment in practices that challenge normative conventions and push for a radical restructuring of the mind.

Acknowledgments

I was inspired to write *Against the Carceral Archive* by the many conversations that I have had over the years with Michele Welsing, Yusef Omowale, and Raquel Chavez—the miraculous caretakers of the Southern California Library. Without question, they have shaped and crafted the contours of my intellectual engagement in a profound way, and for that I am forever in their debt.

The shape and format of the book were also heavily influenced by the time spent going through archival collections alongside Shana Redmond, Dylan Rodríguez, João Costa Vargas, and Stephanie Jones. Their brilliant insight and collective imagining of what a research endeavor could be was beautiful to be a part of, and the lessons learned through that process have been instrumental in the crafting of the book. Thank you also to André Larry, Ayanna Harris, Bree Serna, Diana Gamez, Kristy Hernandez, Anthony Garry, Victor Aviles, and Austen Lawrence, who were instrumental in culling through the collections and engaging in conversations pertaining to the endless possibilities of meaning.

The late Michael Zinzun, cofounder of the Coalition Against Police Abuse, was a central part of this project. I had the opportunity to learn a tremendous amount about organizing strategy and praxis through working alongside him and talking with the people he organized with.

A major thanks to my friends Orisanmi Burton, Sabina Vaught, Kristen Peterson, Sarah Haley, Connie Wun, Dylan Rodriguez, and Valerie Olsen, who constantly championed and supported me to construct and complete the book during some very turbulent times. Thanks so much to Ashon Crawley, SA Smythe, and Sandra Harvey, who at a symposium at the University of California San Diego helped me think much more deeply about the notion of an archive and its capacity as an ongoing project.

I am especially indebted to the editorial staff at the Fordham University Press. Richard Morrison patiently shepherded the book from a collection of ideas to its fully realized form. Always responsive and motivating, Richard has been a dream editor, and I am thankful for all his time and energy on the project. A huge note of thanks to the readers who were extremely generous in their feedback and provided sage advice that was critical in constructing the finer points of the book. Thank you so much to Sofia Pedroza, who copy edited an early version in record time; your skill and effort is truly appreciated.

My sister, Leslie Schnyder, has been simply amazing, and I cannot begin to thank her enough. Godfrey and Elaine Schnyder are the best parents anyone could ask for and have been a consistent foundation throughout the writing of this book.

This was a labor of love that could not have been done without the support of a multitude of colleagues, friends, and family whose names could fill an entire book by themselves. Thank you all for your support, as it has been foundational to the writing of this book.

Finally, this book could not have been written without the love and commitment from Shana, Naima, and Nesanet Sojoyner. Shana has been tremendous in her support through the highs and lows that have occurred throughout the process. I am forever in her debt and thank her a million times over for her kindness and generosity. Naima and Nesanet have been blessings manifested over and over again. They have brought nothing but joy, laughter, and love to my life. Everything I do is for them and my love for them is unwavering.

References

Against the Carceral Archive has been informed by a wide range of sources that have been fundamental to thinking about the archive and organizing against the carceral state. The struggle against the carceral state has an expansive genealogical past whose intellectual and political foundations rest within specific Black epistemes to which this project is forever indebted. As a matter of paying it forward, I offer a collection of sources that have been critical to the study against the carceral state and pontifications upon the archive and the archival. This offering is not meant to be inclusive of all the works pertaining to carceral struggle or the archival, but rather is a contribution to Black study and thought.

Abraham, J. 1975. "Los Angeles Police Department Emergency Command Control Communication System (Phase I, Task III) Mobile Digital System Specification." Report for Los Angeles Police Department 1200–246. Jet Propulsion Laboratory. Box 10, Folder 18. Southern California Library: Coalition Against Police Abuse Collection.

Abu-Jamal, Mumia. 1996. *Live from Death Row*. Introduction by John Edgar Wideman. New York: Harper Perennial.

———. 2016. *We Want Freedom: A Life in the Black Panther Party*. Introduction by Kathleen Cleaver. New ed. Brooklyn, NY: Common Notions.

Aerospace Corporation. 1970. "Evaluation of the Proposed Tactical Information Correlation and Retrieval System (PATRIC)." Southern California Library: Coalition Against Police Abuse Collection.

Alcorn, Brian. 1995. "Jaws of the Law: Police Dogs as Deadly Force." *LA Weekly*, February 10, 1995. Southern California Library: Urban Policy Research Institute Collection.

Allen, Mark. 1977. "James E. Carter and the Trilateral Commission: A Southern Strategy." *Black Scholar* 8 (7): 2–7.

Allen, Robert L. 1990. *Black Awakening in Capitalist America: An Analytic History*. Trenton, NJ: Africa World.

American Civil Liberties Union of Southern California. n.d. "Police Malpractice and the Watts Riot." American Civil Liberties Union. Southern California Library: Coalition Against Police Abuse Collection.

Barrs, Rick. 1996. "The Crack Masters: Oscar Danilo Blandon Reyes. This Man and Other Shadowy Figures Infected L.A. with a Crack Epidemic. They Did It to Raise Money for the Contras. And the CIA May Have Helped." *New Times: Los Angeles*, September 12–18. Box 3, Folder 21. Southern California Library: Coalition Against Police Abuse Collection.

Beckwith, George, and Richard Lickhalter. 1976. "Considerations in Local Distribution of Criminal Justice Information." Systems Development Corporation. Box 10, Folder 14. Southern California Library: Coalition Against Police Abuse Collection.

Birmele, Dick. 1971. "County Limitations on Acting as 'Sponsor' for Private Agency Applications for CCCJ Funding." Southern California Library: Urban Policy Research Institute Collection.

Black Panther Party. 1969. "Feeding Hungry Children vs. Men of the Cloth." *Black Panther Intercommunal News Service*, October

25, 1969. Box 4. Southern California Library: Los Angeles Black
Panther Party Collection.

———. 1970a. "Free Lance Bell." *Black Panther Intercommunal News
Service,* January 10, 1970. Box 4. Southern California Library: Los
Angeles Black Panther Party Collection.

———. 1970b. "Battlecry of Medicine." *Black Panther Intercommunal
News Service,* May 19, 1970. Box 4. Southern California Library:
Los Angeles Black Panther Party Collection.

———. 1971a. "The Grand Opening of the Bobby Seale People's
Free Health Clinic." Black Panther Party, Berkeley Branch. Box 1,
Folder 3. Southern California Library: Los Angeles Black Panther
Party Collection.

———. 1971b. "Silent Epidemic." *Black Panther Intercommunal News
Service,* October 23, 1971. Box 4. Southern California Library: Los
Angeles Black Panther Party Collection.

———. 1972a. "This Will Tide Me Over: 16,000 United for Survival."
Black Panther Intercommunal News Service, April 8, 1972. Box 4.

———. 1972b. "20,000 Blacks Vote to Control Hospital: Winston-
Salem Black Community Unites to Keep Hospital Facility."
Black Panther Intercommunal News Service, April 22, 1972. Box 4.
Southern California Library: Los Angeles Black Panther Party
Collection.

Black Panther Party: Southern California Chapter. 1969a. "Pigs Try
Pigs." *Black Panther Community Newsletter,* August 11, 1969, no. 3
edition. Box 1, Folder 3. Southern California Library: Los Angeles
Black Panther Party Collection.

———. 1969b. "Watts Summer Festival: 1969." *Black Panther
Community Newsletter,* August 11, 1969, no. 3 edition. Box 1, Folder
3. Southern California Library: Los Angeles Black Panther Party
Collection.

Board of Police Commissioners. 1976. "Standards and Procedures for
the Los Angeles Department: Public Intelligence Division Files."
Los Angeles: Board of Police Commissioners. Southern California
Library: Urban Policy Research Institute Collection.

Browne, Simone. 2015. *Dark Matters: On the Surveillance of Blackness.*

Durham, NC: Duke University Press. https://doi.org/ 10.1515/9780822375302.

Burton, Orisanmi. 2018. "Organized Disorder: The New York City Jail Rebellion of 1970." *Black Scholar* 48 (4): 28–42. https://doi.org/10 .1080/00064246.2018.1514925.

———. 2021. "Captivity, Kinship, and Black Masculine Care Work under Domestic Warfare." *American Anthropologist* 123 (3): 621–32. https://doi.org/10.1111/aman.13619.

Caldwell, Michael. 1970. "Oil and Imperialism in East Asia." *Bertrand Russell Peace Foundation*, 3–22.

California Crime Technological Research Foundation (CCTRF). 1970. "Automated Criminal Justice Information and Communication Systems in California." Sacramento, CA. Box 10, Folder 14. Southern California Library: Coalition Against Police Abuse Collection.

CCCJ Staff. 1972. "The Nature and Causes of Campus Unrest." Report by the Riots and Disorders Task Force of the California Council on Criminal Justice. California Council on Criminal Justice. Southern California Library: Urban Policy Research Institute Collection.

Chatterjee, Partha. 2000. *The Partha Chatterjee Omnibus: Nationalist Thought and the Colonial World, The Nation and Its Fragments, A Possible India*. UK ed. New Delhi: Oxford University Press.

Churchill, Mae. 1975a. *Statement to the Los Angeles Police Commission on the Subject of Public Disorder Intelligence Files*. Southern California Library: Urban Policy Research Institute Collection.

———. 1975b. "Preliminary Report: Confidentiality & Intelligence Concerning School Records." Los Angeles, CA: Urban Policy Research Institute. Southern California Library: Urban Policy Research Institute Collection.

———. 1976. "Letter to Board of Police Commissioners, City of Los Angeles: Standards and Procedures of the Public Disorder Intelligence Division, Los Angeles Police Department," November 30, 1976. Southern California Library: Urban Policy Research Institute Collection.

Citizens' Commission on Police Repression. 1979. "Motion for New

Trial in Pratt Case." *Rap Sheet*, November–December 1979. Box 16, Folder 4. Southern California Library: Coalition Against Police Abuse Collection.

———. 1980. "LAPD Spied on City Council." *Rap Sheet*, May 1980. Box 8, Folder N. Southern California Library: Coalition Against Police Abuse Collection.

———. 1981a. "Reagan Soft on Crime: FBI Burglars Get Pardon." *Rap Sheet*, April 1981. Box 16, Folder 3. Southern California Library: Coalition Against Police Abuse Collection.

———. 1981b. "Statement by the Citizens' Commission on Police Repression on the Lawsuit against the Los Angeles Police Department." Box 16, Folder 4. Southern California Library: Coalition Against Police Abuse Collection.

Citizens' Committee of Inquiry into Los Angeles Law Enforcement Intelligence Practices. 1975. "Statement of the Citizens' Committee of Inquiry into Los Angeles Law Enforcement Intelligence Practices concerning the Proposed Standards and Procedures for the Public Disorder Intelligence Division of the Los Angeles Police Department." Southern California Library: Urban Policy Research Institute Collection.

Civil Rights Congress. 1951. *We Charge Genocide: The Historic Petition to the United Nations for Relief from a Crime of the United States Government against the Negro People*. Edited by William L. Patterson. 2nd ed. Civil Rights Congress.

Cooperman, Roslyn, and Women For. 1976. *Testimony before the Los Angeles Board of Police Commissioners on the Proposed Final Version of the Standards and Procedures for the Los Angeles Police Department Public Disorder Intelligence Division Files*. Los Angeles, CA.

Corey, George, and Richard Cohen. 1972. "Domestic Pacification." *Society* 9 (1972): 17–23.

CR10 Publications Collective. 2008. *Abolition Now! Ten Years of Strategy and Struggle against the Prison Industrial Complex*. Oakland, CA: AK.

Crawley, Ashon T. 2017. *Blackpentecostal Breath: The Aesthetics of Possibility*. Commonalities. New York: Fordham University Press.

———. 2022. *Meditation on Abolition*. New York: Haymarket Books.

Crogan, Jim. 1993. "The Svorinichs, LAPD, and the City Attorney: Councilman Caught Up in Triangle." *Random Lengths: Independent Harbor News*, October 13, 1993. Box 3, Folder 16. Southern California Library: Coalition Against Police Abuse Collection.

Davis, Angela Y. 2003. *Are Prisons Obsolete?* New York: Seven Stories.

Davis, Angela Y., Gina Dent, Erica R. Meiners, and Beth E. Richie. 2022. *Abolition. Feminism. Now.* Chicago: Haymarket Books.

Davis, Mike. (1990) 2006. *City of Quartz: Excavating the Future in Los Angeles*. New ed. New York: Verso.

Devereaux, Ryan. 2014. "How the CIA Watched Over the Destruction of Gary Webb." The Intercept, September 25, 2014. https://theintercept.com/2014/09/25/managing-nightmare-cia-media-destruction-gary-webb/.

Drake, St. Clair, and Horace R. Cayton. 1945. *Black Metropolis: A Study of Negro Life in a Northern City*. New York: Harcourt, Brace.

Du Bois, W. E. B. 1998. *Black Reconstruction in America, 1860–1880*. Introduction by David Levering Lewis. 12.2.1997 edition. New York: Free Press.

Felker-Kantor, Max. 2018. *Policing Los Angeles: Race, Resistance, and the Rise of the LAPD*. Justice, Power, and Politics. Chapel Hill: University of North Carolina Press.

Fellows, Jarrette, Jr. 1996. "Sheriff's Affidavit Reveals Muddled Trail: US Government Secrecy Hints of a Coverup." *LA Watts Times*, October 10, 1996. Box 3, Folder 21. Southern California Library: Coalition Against Police Abuse Collection.

Ferguson, Roderick A. 2012. *The Reorder of Things: The University and Its Pedagogies of Minority Difference*. Difference Incorporated. Minneapolis: University of Minnesota Press.

Fogelson, Robert M. 1967. "White on Black: A Critique of the McCone Commission Report on the Los Angeles Riots." *Political Science Quarterly* 82 (3): 337–67. https://doi.org/10.2307/2146769.

Fritsch, Albert, and John Egan. 1973. "Big Oil: A Citizen's Factbook on the Major Oil Companies." Washington, DC: Center for Science in the Public Interest. Box 15, Folder 10. Southern California Library: Coalition Against Police Abuse Collection.

Fuentes, Marisa J. 2016. *Dispossessed Lives: Enslaved Women, Violence, and the Archive.* Early American Studies. Philadelphia: University of Pennsylvania Press.

Gilmore, Ruth Wilson. 1999. "Globalisation and US Prison Growth: From Military Keynesianism to Post-Keynesian Militarism." *Race and Class* 40 (2/3): 171–88.

———. 2007. *Golden Gulag: Prisons, Surplus, Crisis, and Opposition in Globalizing California.* Berkeley: University of California Press.

———. 2022a. *Abolition Geography: Essays towards Liberation.* Edited by Brenna Bhandar and Alberto Toscano. New York: Verso.

———. 2022b. *Change Everything: Racial Capitalism and the Case for Abolition.* Edited by Naomi Murakawa. Chicago: Haymarket Books.

Gordon, Avery F. 2017. *The Hawthorn Archive: Letters from the Utopian Margins.* New York: Fordham University Press.

Grigsby, Juli. 2014. "Grim Sleeper: Gender, Violence, and Reproductive Justice in Los Angeles." PhD diss., University of Texas at Austin.

Haley, Sarah. 2016. *No Mercy Here: Gender, Punishment, and the Making of Jim Crow Modernity.* Justice, Power, and Politics. Chapel Hill: University of North Carolina Press.

Hansen, G. R. 1976. "Automatic Vehicle Monitoring Systems Study: Report of Phase 0." Report for National Science Foundation Vol. 1. Jet Propulsion Laboratory. Box 10, Folder 18. Southern California Library: Coalition Against Police Abuse Collection.

Harney, Stefano, and Fred Moten. 2013. *The Undercommons: Fugitive Planning & Black Study.* Brooklyn, NY: Autonomedia.

Harney, Stefano, Fred Moten, Zun Lee, and Denise Ferreira da Silva. 2021. *All Incomplete.* Colchester, UK: Minor Compositions.

Hartman, Saidiya V. 2007. *Lose Your Mother: A Journey along the Atlantic Slave Route.* New York: Farrar, Straus and Giroux.

———. 2019. *Wayward Lives, Beautiful Experiments: Intimate Histories of Social Upheaval.* New York: W. W. Norton.

Haydon, Brownlee. 1978. "Statement to the Los Angeles Board

of Police Commissioners on the Public Disorder Intelligence Division Audit." Southern California Library: Urban Policy Research Institute Collection.

Haydon, Brownlee, Bob Goe, P. Sterne, W. Parker, and R. Corian. 1974. "Report on School Records Project: Work-In-Progess, Working Plans, May 1, 1974 to September 1, 1974." Report to Children's Defense Fund. Los Angeles: Urban Policy Research Institute. Southern California Library: Urban Policy Research Institute Collection.

Hicks, Cheryl D. 2010. *Talk with You Like a Woman: African American Women, Justice, and Reform in New York, 1890–1935.* Gender and American Culture. Chapel Hill: University of North Carolina Press.

Hill, James N. 1999. "The Committee on Ethics: Past, Present, and Future." In *Handbook on Ethical Issues in Anthropology,* edited by Joan Cassell and Sue-Ellen Jacobs, 11–19. American Anthropological Association special publication no. 23. https://www.americananthro.org/LearnAndTeach/Content .aspx?ItemNumber=12911.

Hodel, Georg. 1997. "Hung Out to Dry: 'Dark Alliance' Series Dies." *Consortium for Independent Journalism,* June 20, 1997, vol. 2, no. 15. Box 5, Folder 23. Southern California Library: Coalition Against Police Abuse Collection.

Holland, Randy. n.d. *The Fire This Time.* Documentary.

Horne, Gerald. 1997. *Fire This Time: The Watts Uprising and the 1960s.* New York: Da Capo.

Hunn, Nova. 1997. "Coalition Protests Police Brutality." *Wave,* September 17, 1997. Box 5, Folder 13. Southern California Library: Coalition Against Police Abuse Collection.

Illinois Black Panther Party, Young Lords Organizations, and SDS. n.d. "The Struggle for Freedom in Chicago and Vietnam." Box 1, Folder 6. Southern California Library: Los Angeles Black Panther Party Collection.

Jackson, George. (1970) 1994. *Soledad Brother: The Prison Letters of George Jackson.* Foreword by Jonathan Jackson Jr.; introduction by Jean Genet. New ed. Chicago: Lawrence Hill Books.

Jackson, George L. (1972) 1996. *Blood in My Eye*. Reprint, Baltimore, MD: Black Classic.

James, Joy, ed. 2003. *Imprisoned Intellectuals: America's Political Prisoners Write on Life, Liberation, and Rebellion*. Lanham, MD: Rowman and Littlefield.

———, ed. 2005. *The New Abolitionists:* Unabridged ed. Albany: State University of New York Press.

———, ed. 2007. *Warfare in the American Homeland: Policing and Prison in a Penal Democracy*. Durham, NC: Duke University Press.

Jentzsch, Heber. 1977. "40 Million Dollar Rip Off." *Los Angeles Free Press*, 1977. Box 10, Folder 18. Southern California Library: Coalition Against Police Abuse Collection.

Joint Legislative Audit Committee. 1972. "California Criminal Justice Information System." Sacramento: California Legislature.

Kaba, Mariame 2021. *We Do This 'Til We Free Us: Abolitionist Organizing and Transforming Justice*. Edited by Tamara K. Nopper. Foreword by Naomi Murakawa. Chicago: Haymarket Books.

Kaba, Mariame, and Andrea Ritchie. 2022. *No More Police: A Case for Abolition*. New York: New Press.

Kelley, Robin D. G. 1996. *Race Rebels: Culture, Politics, and the Black Working Class*. New York: Free Press.

Law Enforcement Assistance Administration Emergency Energy Committee. 1974. "Preliminary Report on Crime and the Energy Crises." Washington, DC: United States Department of Justice. Box 15, Folder 10. Southern California Library: Coalition Against Police Abuse Collection.

Lawson, Robert W., and Ralph W. Lanz. 1974. "Reports from Law-Enforcement Agencies concerning Pupils Arrested for Narcotics Violations." Los Angeles, CA: Los Angeles Unified School District: Division of Educational Support Services. Southern California Library: Urban Policy Research Institute Collection.

Lynn, Janice. 1979. "Stop US Threats against Iran!" *The Militant: A Socialist Newsweekly Published in the Interests of the Working People*, November 16, 1979. Box 4, Folder 13. Southern California Library: Coalition Against Police Abuse Collection.

McDonald, Greg. 1980. "Socialist Group Says FBI Spying Led to

Lockheed Firings." *Atlanta Journal*, December 18, 1980, Thursday Evening ed. Box 4, Folder 13. Southern California Library: Coalition Against Police Abuse Collection.

McKittrick, Katherine, ed. 2015. *Sylvia Wynter: On Being Human as Praxis*. Durham, NC: Duke University Press.

McKittrick, Katherine, and Clyde Woods, eds. 2007. *Black Geographies and the Politics of Place*. Cambridge, MA: South End.

Mehrotra, Dhruv, Surya Mattu, Annie Gilbertson, and Aaron Sankin. 2021. "How We Determined Predictive Policing Software Disproportionately Targeted Low-Income, Black, and Latino Neighborhoods." Gizmodo. Accessed May 18, 2022. https://gizmodo.com/how-we-determined-predictive-policing-software-dispropo-1848139456.

Meiners, Erica R. 2016. *For the Children? Protecting Innocence in a Carceral State*. Minneapolis: University of Minnesota Press.

Millennials Are Killing Capitalism (blog). n.d. "'We Cannot Allow Our Movement to Abandon Them in Prison'—Jalil Muntaqim on Political Prisoners, Charging Genocide and Organizing Inside & Out." Accessed May 25, 2022. https://millennialsarekillingcapitalism.libsyn.com/we-cannot-allow-our-movement-to-abandon-them-in-prison-jalil-muntaqim-on-political-prisoners-charging-genocide-and-organizing-inside-out.

Miller, Alan S. 1972. *The Case of the People against Standard Oil*. San Francisco, CA: Pacific Counseling Service.

Momjian, Edmond. 1974. "Advanced Command and Control Systems for Law Enforcement." Jet Propulsion Laboratory. Box 10, Folder 18. Southern California Library: Coalition Against Police Abuse Collection.

Muntaqim, Jalil A. 2010. *We Are Our Own Liberators: Selected Prison Writings*. 2nd ed. Portland, OR: Arissa Media Group.

MVD Entertainment Group, Setsu Shigematsu, and Cameron Granadino. 2012. *Visions of Abolition: From Critical Resistance to a New Way of Life*. VAST: Academic Video Online. Pottstown, PA: MVD Entertainment Group.

Oliver, Melvin, and W. C. Farrell. 1993. "Anatomy of a Rebellion: A Political-Economic Analysis." In *Reading Rodney King / Reading*

Urban Uprising, edited by Robert Gooding-Williams. New York: Routledge.

Olsen, Jack. (2000) 2001. *Last Man Standing: The Tragedy and Triumph of Geronimo Pratt*. Reprint, New York: Anchor.

Ortiz, Paul. 2000. "The Anatomy of a Rebellion." *Against the Current* 84 (January/February). https://againstthecurrent.org/atc084/p1696/.

Osuna, Steven. 2019. "The Psycho Realm Blues: The Violence of Policing, Disordering Practices, and Rap Criticism in Los Angeles." *Chiricú* 4 (1): 76–100. https://doi.org/10.2979/chiricu.4.1.06.

Outcry: Independent New Left Weekly. 1979. "Abortion: Prison Style." April 22, 1979, sec. Toward a Women's Movement. Box 1, Folder 17. Southern California Library: Los Angeles Black Panther Party Collection.

Parry, Robert. 1996. "Antifa Info-Bulletin: The CIA, Contras and Crack." *Consortium for Independent Journalism*, September 8, 1996. Box 8, Folder N. Southern California Library: Coalition Against Police Abuse Collection.

Prison Policy Initiative, and Peter Wagner and Wendy Sawyer. 2018. "Mass Incarceration: The Whole Pie 2018." Prison Policy Initiative. https://www.prisonpolicy.org/reports/pie2018.html.

Richie, Beth E. 2012. *Arrested Justice: Black Women, Violence, and America's Prison Nation*. New York: New York University Press.

Ritchie, Andrea J. 2017. *Invisible No More: Police Violence against Black Women and Women of Color*. Foreword by Angela Y. Davis. Boston: Beacon.

Riveria, Michael. 2020. "How Can We Problematize White Supremacy, Mass Incarceration and Police Violence?" *The Arch & Anth Podcast*. Accessed May 25, 2022. https://archandanth.com/episode-136-interview-with-orisanmi-burton/.

Robinson, Cedric J. 2021. *Black Marxism: The Making of the Black Radical Tradition*. Foreword by Robin D. G. Kelley. Preface by Damien Sojoyner and Tiffany Willoughby-Herard. 3rd ed. Chapel Hill: University of North Carolina Press.

———. 2007. *Forgeries of Memory and Meaning: Blacks and the*

Regimes of Race in American Theater and Film before World War II.
Chapel Hill: University of North Carolina Press.

———. 2016. *The Terms of Order: Political Science and the Myth of Leadership.* New foreword by Erica R. Edwards. Chapel Hill: University of North Carolina Press.

———. 2019. *An Anthropology of Marxism.* Preface by Avery F. Gordon. New foreword by H. L. T. Quan. 2nd ed. Chapel Hill: University of North Carolina Press.

Robinson, William I., and Cesar Rodriguez. 2020. "Militarised Accumulation." *Journal of Australian Political Economy,* no. 86: 256–79.

Rockwell, Joanne W. 1971. "The California Criminal Justice System." California Council on Criminal Justice. Southern California Library: Urban Policy Research Institute Collection.

Rodríguez, Dylan. 2006. *Forced Passages: Imprisoned Radical Intellectuals and the U.S. Prison Regime.* Minneapolis: University of Minnesota Press.

———. 2007. "The Political Logic of the Non-profit Industrial Complex." In *The Revolution Will Not Be Funded: Beyond the Non-profit Industrial Complex,* edited by INCITE!, 21–40. Cambridge, MA: South End.

———. 2021. *White Reconstruction: Domestic Warfare and the Logics of Genocide.* New York: Fordham University Press. https://doi .org/10.1515/9780823289417.

Schept, Judah. 2022. *Coal, Cages, Crisis: The Rise of the Prison Economy in Central Appalachia.* New York: New York University Press.

Schrader, Stuart. 2019. *Badges without Borders: How Global Counterinsurgency Transformed American Policing.* American Crossroads 56. Berkeley: University of California Press. https:// doi.org/10.1525/9780520968332.

Shakur, Assata. 2001. *Assata: An Autobiography.* Chicago: Lawrence Hill Books.

Sharpe, Christina Elizabeth. 2016. *In the Wake: On Blackness and Being.* Durham, NC: Duke University Press.

Shields, Hannah, and Mae Churchill. 1974. "The Younger They Are, the Harder They Fall." Report by the Urban Policy Research

Institute. Southern California Library: Urban Policy Research
Institute Collection.

Sloan, Cle, dir. 2005. *Bastards of the Party*. Documentary film. http://
www.imdb.com/title/tt0455913/.

Spivak, Gayatri Chakravorty. 1999. *A Critique of Postcolonial Reason:
Toward a History of the Vanishing Present*. Cambridge, MA:
Harvard University Press.

Stanley, Tom, and Los Angeles Center for Law & Justice. 1979.
"Complaint about Public Disorder Intelligence Division at
Hearing into Eula Love Shooting." May 11, 1979. Box 16, Folder
6. Southern California Library: Coalition Against Police Abuse
Collection.

Sterne, Pat. 1975. "Description of Drug Survey, Undercover
Operation, Arrests." Urban Policy Research Institute. Southern
California Library: Urban Policy Research Institute Collection.

Sutherland, Tonia. 2019. "The Carceral Archive: Documentary
Records, Narrative Construction, and Predictive Risk
Assessment." *Journal of Cultural Analytics*, June 4, 2019. https://
doi.org/10.22148/16.039.

Sweet, Cassandra. 1997. "Reporter Says He's Been Pulled Off Story,
Transferred." *Associated Press*, June 12, 1997. Box 5, Folder 23.
Southern California Library: Coalition Against Police Abuse
Collection.

Tanzer, Michael. 1974. "The International Oil Crisis: A Tightrope
between Depression and War." *Social Policy* 5 (4): 23–29.

Thomas, Deborah A. 2019. *Political Life in the Wake of the Plantation:
Sovereignty, Witnessing, Repair*. Illustrated ed. Durham, NC: Duke
University Press.

Thomas, Vincent, and William Merrifield. 1972. "Report on the
California Criminal Justice Information System." Report to
California Assembly Select Committee on the Administration of
Justice. Sacramento, CA: Joint Legislative Audit Committee.

Thuma, Emily L. 2019. *All Our Trials: Prisons, Policing, and the
Feminist Fight to End Violence*. Urbana: University of Illinois Press.

Tomlinson, T. O., and David Sears. 1967. "Los Angeles Riot Study:
Negro Attitudes toward the Riot." Los Angeles: Institute of

Government and Public Affairs, Department of Psychology, University of California, Los Angeles. Southern California Library: Urban Policy Research Institute Collection.

"TransformHarm.org | Welcome | A Resource Hub about Ending Violence." n.d. Transform Harm. Accessed May 18, 2022. https://transformharm.org/.

Trouillot, Michel-Rolph. 2003. "Anthropology and the Savage Slot: The Poetics and Politics of Otherness." In *Global Transformations: Anthropology and the Modern World*, by Michel-Rolph Trouillot, 7–28. New York: Palgrave Macmillan US. https://doi.org/10.1007/978-1-137-04144-9_2.

———. 2015. *Silencing the Past: Power and the Production of History*. ACLS Humanities E-Book (Series). Boston: Beacon.

Vargas, João H. Costa. 2004. "The Los Angeles Times' Coverage of the 1992 Rebellion: Still Burning Matters of Race and Justice." *Ethnicities* 4 (2): 209–36. https://doi.org/10.1177/1468796804042604.

———. 2006. *Catching Hell in the City of Angels: Life and Meanings of Blackness in South Central Los Angeles*. Minneapolis: University of Minnesota Press. https://www.upress.umn.edu/book-division/books/catching-hell-in-the-city-of-angels.

Vaught, Sabina E. 2017. *Compulsory: Education and the Dispossession of Youth in a Prison School*. Minneapolis: University of Minnesota Press.

Vitale, Alex S. 2021. *The End of Policing*. Updated ed. New York: Verso.

Volkman, Ernest. 1980. "Othello (Helped the FBI Destroy Legitimate Political Dissent in the United States)." *Penthouse*, April 1980. Box 8, Folder N. Southern California Library: Coalition Against Police Abuse Collection.

Walcott, Rinaldo. 2021. *On Property: Policing, Prisons, and the Call for Abolition*. Windsor, ON: Biblioasis.

Wilson, Bobby M. 2019. *America's Johannesburg: Industrialization and Racial Transformation in Birmingham*. 2000. Reprint, Athens: University of Georgia Press.

Wolf, Eric R., and Joseph G. Jorgensen. 1970. "A Special Supplement: Anthropology on the Warpath in Thailand." *New*

York Review, November 19, 1970. https://www.nybooks.com/articles/1970/11/19/a-special-supplement-anthropology-on-the-warpath-i/.

Woods, Clyde. 2017. *Development Arrested: The Blues and Plantation Power in the Mississippi Delta*. 2nd ed. New York: Verso.

Workers Vanguard. 1979. "Smash KKK Killers." November 9, 1979, no. 243 edition, sec. Labor/Black Mass Mobilizations. Box 4, Folder 13. Southern California Library: Coalition Against Police Abuse Collection.

Wynter, Sylvia. 1976. "Ethno or Socio Poetics." *Alcheringa: Ethnopoetics* 2 (2): 78–94.

———. 1979. "Sambos and Minstrels." *Social Text*, no. 1 (Winter): 149–56. https://doi.org/10.2307/466410.

———. 1984. "The Ceremony Must Be Found: After Humanism." *Boundary 2* 12/13 (Spring–Autumn): 19–70. https://doi.org/10.2307/302808.

———. 2003. "Unsettling the Coloniality of Being/Power/Truth/Freedom: Towards the Human, After Man, Its Overrepresentation—An Argument." *CR: The New Centennial Review* 3 (3): 257–337. https://doi.org/10.1353/ncr.2004.0015.

Damien M. Sojoyner is Associate Professor in the Department of Anthropology at the University of California, Irvine. He is the author of *First Strike: Educational Enclosures in Black Los Angeles* (University of Minnesota Press, 2016) and *Joy and Pain: A Story of Black Life and Liberation in Five Albums* (University of California Press, 2022).